Extraordinary
TEACHERS

Teaching for Success

Extraordinary
TEACHERS
Teaching for Success

MICHAEL WHITE

AMY CROUSE

CARA BAFILE

HARRY BARNES

LEAD+
LEARN
PRESS

The Leadership and Learning Center
317 Inverness Way South, Suite 150, Englewood, Colorado 80112
Phone 1.866.399.6019 | Fax 303.504.9417 | LeadandLearn.com

Published by Lead+Learn Press, a division of Advanced Learning Centers, Inc.

All Web links in this book are correct as of the publication date below, but may have become inactive or otherwise modified since that time. If you notice a deactivated or changed link, please notify the publisher and specify the Web link, the book title, and the page number on which the link appears so that corrections may be made in future editions.

Lead+Learn Press also publishes books in a variety of electronic formats. Some content that appears in print may not be available in electronic books.

11 10 09 08 01 02 03 04 05 06 07 08 09

ISBN 978-1-933196-92-3

Library of Congress Cataloging-in-Publication Data

White, Michael.
    Extraordinary teachers : teaching for success / by Michael White ... [et al.].
        p. cm.
    Includes bibliographical references and index.
    ISBN 978-1-933196-92-3
    1. Teachers. 2. Effective teaching. 3. Teacher effectiveness. I. Title.
    LB1775.W47 2009
    371.1--dc22
                                2009015864

DEDICATION

Our heartfelt appreciation is extended to the best teachers
we have ever met: Doug, Nikki, Chris, Dana, Tim, Dee, Don,
Katherine, T.J., Libby, Louis, Emma, Wes, Teresa, Natalie, Dustin,
Glen, Phyllis, Jeff, Lindsey, Sarah, LeeAnn, and Kelly.

Contents

About the Authors

Michael White is a professional development associate with the Leadership and Learning Center and the director of Educational Consulting Services, an educational organization in Cincinnati, Ohio. He is also a licensed pediatric psychologist.

Dr. White consults with school systems throughout the country on issues relating to standards-based instruction and assessment. A strong advocate of "assessment as instruction," he is the author of three books and numerous articles on standards, assessment, and effective schools. His web-based teacher resource, Learning Connection Online, was the National Staff Development Council's Technology of the Year award winner for 2003.

His books and presentations are the result of his work with small rural school districts, suburban school districts, and urban school districts throughout the country and are grounded in twenty-five years of teaching and coaching experience.

Amy Crouse is the director of curriculum and instruction for Princeton City Schools in Cincinnati, Ohio. Her resume includes being a classroom teacher at the primary level through middle school, a middle school assistant principal, and an elementary principal. She has worked in a variety of settings, cities, and states, giving her a wide perspective of experiences upon which to draw. Her ideas are grounded in real-life application to teachers. Her work is guided by the belief that quality teaching comes from teachers growing and learning together to improve student learning.

Crouse earned her BA from Indiana University and her MEd in educational administration from the University of Cincinnati. She lives and plays in Cincinnati with her husband and three children.

Cara Bafile is a freelance writer who has authored and edited education-related books, articles, and classroom materials for ten years. She is a columnist for the monthly *Classroom Connect* newsletter and writes weekly and bi-weekly features and full-length articles that appear online through publications such as *Education World* (http://www.educationworld.com).

As a former kindergarten teacher, Bafile seeks to share the most practical and useful information of interest to new and established teachers. She obtained a BA in elementary education from the University of Pittsburgh at Johnstown and currently resides in Mercersburg, Pennsylvania, with her husband and two children.

Harry Barnes attended the University of Cincinnati, where he earned a bachelor's degree in education and a master's degree in school psychology. He also attended Xavier University (Cincinnati), where he earned administrative certification. He has more than thirty-four years of experience in education, with a resume that includes the titles of author, special education coordinator, assistant principal, and principal. Presently, he is a school psychologist in an urban school district, and an educational consultant for Urban Renewal Educational Services. In addition, as a principal coach in a large urban school district, he mentored principals and implemented schoolwide improvement plans.

Foreword

Larry Ainsworth

Extraordinary Teachers: Teaching for Success, written by educators for educators, is a how-to instruction manual filled with research-supported, practical, and proven advice. After reading this book, new and not-so-new teachers will enter the halls of learning with a wide array of tools needed to face the challenges ahead of them.

I wish I had a book like this when I started my teaching career 35 years ago. I could have saved myself so much anguish and done an infinitely better job for my students. Instead, I was left to discover these gems of collective wisdom on my own in the "school of hard knocks."

The scope of the book is ambitious; it needs to be. As anyone who has ever set foot in a classroom can attest, there are many critically important elements that you must understand and simultaneously deal with. This book gives both new and veteran teachers innovative and effective ways of doing so. Highlights include:

- Personnel tips ("Always remember that your best friends are the secretary and custodian. Treat them with dignity!")

- Classroom-management advice (time management, calendar usage, routines, substitutes, etc.)

- Instruction and assessment processes (prioritizing the standards, creating hands-on classroom performance assessments, engaging students through meaningful goal-setting, tackling the grading dilemma, etc.)

- Implementation of powerful professional practices (Data Teams and professional learning communities).

The authors do a wonderful job of "introducing" us to some teaching colleagues, and their diverse personalities, that we are likely to encounter. In Steph, Ken, Kay, and Ira we see dedicated educational professionals with varying degrees of effective teaching practices. These players become our guides as they provide us with excellent suggestions for establishing all-important relationships with students, parents, and colleagues.

Once we know who our stakeholders are, we move on to the actual day-to-day work of teaching, student learning, and assessment, through accessible and plain language that is consistently engaging and often inspiring. Using the journal activities, you will be able to process, and more importantly, immediately apply the ideas presented here. Be sure to note all the tools to help busy educators "work smarter, not harder," such as Web sites that provide templates to make preparation easier, along with great suggestions for involving both students and parents. As a bonus, the appendices at the end of the book are filled with useful forms and templates to help us busy teachers everywhere.

The authors temper this clear and concise work for busy practitioners with inspiring language that reminds us why we sought this path in the first place:

> "The whole world is watching as we provide more complex instruction,
> covering a wider range of skills, to an increasingly diverse group of students.
> It is not these challenges that will define our generation of teachers, however—
> but our response."

> "Keep your eye on test scores and Adequate Yearly Progress data, but never lose
> your sense of wonder with the children entrusted to you each school year."

Like that great mentor I never had, *Extraordinary Teachers* is encouraging and supportive, never once overwhelming by urging us to implement all the helpful recommendations at once. Even the closing call to action underscores that idea— that, by perseverance, you can surely become extraordinary over time. "We have the opportunity to take education to a higher level—to do something extraordinary! People are not born extraordinary. Extraordinary comes and finds you. It's in what you do next—how you respond to a situation or a challenge."

Introduction

Teachers, Students, and Standards

This world of higher standards, No Child Left Behind (NCLB), international competition, student diversity, and public scrutiny present teachers with a huge challenge and is changing the very nature of education. The challenge grows out of the promise teachers have made to deliver a world-class education fairly, rather than tolerate low-level instruction or persistent gaps in student learning. The whole world is watching as we provide more complex instruction, covering a wider range of skills, to an increasingly diverse group of students. It is not these challenges that will define our generation of teachers, however—but our response.

We have the opportunity to take education to a higher level—to do something extraordinary! People are not born extraordinary. Extraordinary comes and finds you. It's in what you do next—how you respond to a situation or a challenge. Some people choose to run away, some remain but do almost nothing, while some choose to act. It's our hope that in some small way the following pages energize you to *act*.

The good news is that we are up to the challenge. Over the past few years, the academic qualifications of teachers have risen dramatically. A recent study conducted by Educational Testing Services found that:

- The SAT-Verbal scores for new teachers have increased by thirteen points over the past eight years; SAT-Math scores have increased by seventeen points.

- The percentage of new teachers reporting higher than a 3.5 GPA has increased from 27 to 40 over the past eight years, while the percentage of new teachers reporting lower than a 3.0 GPA has decreased from 32 to 20.

- These improvements are consistent across genders, racial/ethnic groups, and licensure areas (Gitomor 2007).

So you are off to a great start, and you know that you will continually develop new knowledge and skills. This book provides a framework for that new knowledge and will generate thoughtful reflection and discussion about how extraordinary teachers teach and all students learn. We don't aspire to take the place of Doug Reeves, Bob Marzano, or Harry Wong on your bookshelf. We do not pretend to have the answers. In fact, we believe that you have all the answers you need. This book was written to help you find them within your community, within your students, and within yourself.

The first section of the book deals with people—the players. We'll present some advice and examples for getting the most out of interactions with your colleagues, the parents of your students, and, most importantly, your students. In the second part of the book, we shift the context from people to the plan. We'll take some enormously powerful teaching ideas and present them in a manner that can be used by anyone without benefit of an interpreter or an advanced degree in educational research or statistical analysis.

Always remember (we certainly did while writing this book): The challenge is to become an extraordinary, standards-based teacher without losing the tenderness, perhaps even the mischievousness, that brought you to this profession. Keep your eye on test scores and Adequate Yearly Progress (AYP) data, but never lose your sense of wonder with the children entrusted to you each school year.

Undoubtedly, you will hear a small handful of your colleagues complaining about standards, state testing, and NCLB. You'll hear stories about the good old days of public school and wonder if you missed out on what must have been education nirvana. Don't be fooled. The truth is, the good old days were not good for everybody. Here's our version of a story that Larry Lezotte shares with teachers all over the country:

Once upon a time, schools were places where most of the children were alike; two parents, a dog or cat, and a three-bedroom house. The students were taught by teachers who looked like this, too. Together they walked in straight lines down the halls, learned, sang, and were polite. It was a wonderful place and a wonderful time. Some folks said it always smelled like cookies. It was called Public School Way Back When (PSWBW).

Everyone was happy because they knew PSWBW was running smoothly. The principals were very happy. Their job was to keep the rain out and the students in. Attendance was mandatory; learning was optional. After all, "Some kids had it and some didn't." Teachers were happy, too. The job of PSWBW wasn't to have all of the students achieve at the same level. The job of PSWBW was to sort students into three groups: leaders, workers, and a few extra students at the bottom (bless their hearts).

The leaders would go on to college, become executives, and own factories and businesses. The workers would get jobs on the assembly line and in the warehouses of these factories. And if anyone needed anything else, there was always the small group of extra people. PSWBW called this plan the normal curve.

The leaders needed to be able to think deep thoughts. Things ran smoother if the workers did not think deep thoughts. The last thing a customer would want was a car or a toaster that was rolling down the assembly line just when a worker stepped back to say, "You know boys, I've been thinking . . ."

There was some diversity among the PSWBW student body, but it was an obstacle that could be overcome. Over time, new students were assimilated, and those with different cultural and ethnic backgrounds were "Americanized." Placing these students in their assigned groups was

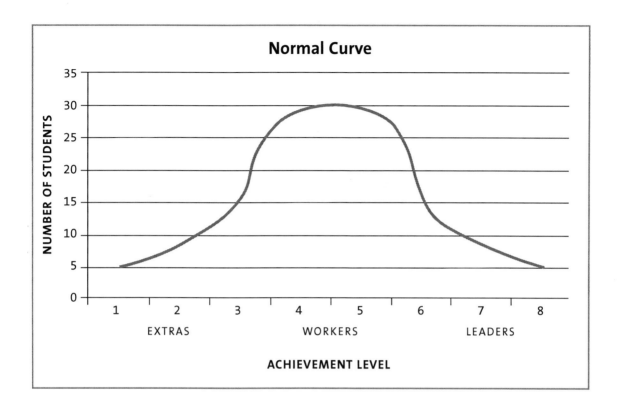

a simple matter: *Did they speak the language correctly and could they read it? If not, to the "extras" they went. The normal curve was so pleasant that maintaining it became the goal.*

PSWBW operated like this for a long time, but gradually things changed. Maybe it was when the leaders decided to use machines on their assembly lines. Maybe things changed when the leaders decided to move their factories to other countries and use those workers to build things.

Maybe things changed because workers and extras decided that they wanted to learn to be leaders, too. The truth is, no one really felt all that comfortable about how those extra students were being treated.

One thing was certain: The numbers of PSWBW's "extra" students were growing. Diversity increased as immigrants from other cities, states, and countries enrolled their children in the school. More cultures and more races were represented. The children came from many different socioeconomic backgrounds. It wasn't as easy to identify the leaders, the workers, or the extra students. And more diversity was expected in the future.

Folks decided to change the way PSWBW did business. No more "blue bird" and "red bird" reading groups. No more normal curve or extra students. Everyone would be taught to be a leader. In the new No Child Left Behind public schools (NCLBPS), all students would be expected and helped to learn the same things. These things would be called standards. The normal curve, which probably wasn't normal at all, was tossed out and a new curve was invented. It was called the J curve. The J curve showed that all students can learn to be leaders and that no student should be extra.

You have a choice: You can resent and resist standards, the spotlight, and those somewhat clunky state tests, or you can celebrate what could be education's greatest moment and the chance to change the world for millions of "extra" children.

Celebrate, but quickly, and let's change their world this school year!

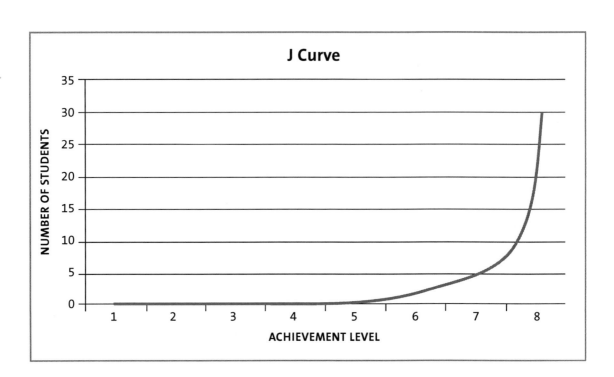

SECTION 1

The Players

Your Colleagues

If we require children to get along and be friendly, courteous, and respectful, shouldn't we expect similar behavior of grown-ups? Some will roll their eyes and argue that a discussion of people skills is just education blather. It's not! A mountain of research shows that people skills and work relationships account for nearly three times as much success in any organization than technical skills (Goleman *et. al.* 2002). And the price tag for people avoiding malcontents, looking for other jobs, and eventually leaving for those other jobs can exceed $50,000 per employee per year across all jobs in the United States (Morse 2005).

So, arrive at your school with a smile on your face. Meet and greet everyone. Do not save your best attitude and charm for licensed colleagues and administrators. The best teachers treat everyone as peers and partners in their work.

Always remember that your best friends are the secretary and custodian. They can find you anything and help you navigate everything. Bring them chocolate. Make them smile. Treat them with dignity! Their first impression of you is nearly as important as what the children think of you.

Your smile and friendliness are important parts of your reputation and education. In larger districts especially, your reputation will help get you selected for key committee work that will broaden your influence and stretch your intellect.

Who's Who in Your Building?

Throughout your teaching career, you'll meet people with a wide range of personalities: some will be complementary to your own, others will just grate on your nerves. In order to maintain peace in the workplace, and for the sake of your own sanity, you need to learn how to deal with people whom you might prefer to place on home instruction. Obviously, this takes practice and patience on your part. The combinations of personality types out there are vast and varied. Our experience has led us to see some patterns in people's behaviors. The following caricatures are designed to help you recognize some of these patterns in your colleagues and yourself.

SCOOP

It may take time for you to like some of your colleagues, and let's be honest—there will be people with whom you may never become friends. But they don't know what you are feeling or thinking. They only know what you say and do. So fake it 'til you make it, and don't get pulled into gossip or bad-mouthing of colleagues.

Steph Uneedtono is the person who loves the students and the school and helping everyone in it. Her compassion, civility, and genuineness can make her the hub of the building. She may not have an advanced degree or be at the top of the pay scale. She probably is not an administrator and may not even be a teacher.

Do you need to know how to get a master key so that you can work in your classroom over the weekend? Ask Steph. Do you need to find someone to teach you how to use the on-line attendance system? Ask Steph. Who organizes the sunshine fund and the birthday list? What days do folks go to happy hour? Ask Steph.

It is equally important to discover Ken Tankerous. Ken can be toxic. Although he may have some solid teaching and classroom-management skills, he likes to speak first, speak loudly, and speak long. He is often disrespectful, and behaves as though everyone's primary concern should be to make his life easier. He complains that he is tired, underpaid, and disrespected. Ken believes that professional development is the perfect time to catch up on magazine reading, grading papers, or napping. And he acts as if those workshop seats at the front of the room are reserved for the bride's family. He usually starts sentences with the phrase, "kids nowadays," or "if we're going to prepare them for the real world." Ken will sacrifice relationships for rigor. He will set the bar high, but will fail to support students in reaching that bar. Ken believes in the normal curve and designs his instruction to achieve that curve. Ken expects all students to know how to behave in his class because they "should know that by now." Ken's survival strategy is to wait out the current administration. His mantra is, "This initiative, too, shall pass." Don't get on his bad side, and don't let him sour you on your career, your colleagues, or your class.

Then there's Kay Serra. Kay is child-centered and caring. Her room smells like cookies, and some days you'll swear you see a rainbow in it. There is laughter and smiling faces and hugs for everyone. Kay's philosophy is about building relationships with students and families. She is often requested by parents, and has a reputation of loving the hardest-to-love students. Admirable qualities to be sure! The problem with Kay Serra is that she doesn't have a sense of urgency for teaching the standards. Kay will not complete her morning meeting time until every student has had the opportunity to share their weekend success on the soccer/baseball/football field. She will personally mediate every playground scuffle through to the sincere apology and action plan for the following day. Kay will have the class develop the rules, but she will not consistently enforce them. There will always be special circumstances. Kay will have students create elaborate Mother's Day planters and papier-mâché pumpkins to die for. Students can and will divert Kay's teaching daily, and soon they will fall far behind the academic plan created for that grade level. Kay Serra will always sacrifice rigor for relationships and, therefore, will miss the opportunity to use her relationships to build understanding and learning about standards.

Be on the Lookout for Iras

After discovering your Stephs, Kens, and Kays, be on the lookout for Ira Flect. Ira is a remarkable teacher who humbly approaches each day with urgency and passion. There is not a formula for extraordinary teaching ... two parts Marzano, one part Leno, shake and bake. Educational and psychological research presents a menu of teaching strategies that have demonstrated a very good chance of making you extraordinary—most of the time. These tips make up the science of effective teaching. Ira knows when to use these tips, and he knows the right student with whom to use them. That's the art of teaching!

Watch and learn how Ira Flect divides the material into small chunks, divides the students into small groups, checks for learning, and makes adjustments. Ira doesn't always have all students at the proficient level, but Ira has a nose for finding those who aren't and, for making mid-unit

corrections. He celebrates his successes, big and small, analyzes his failures, and reflects on the lessons he learned. His lesson plans aren't laminated, because he's always refining them.

Ira will not be as easily recognized as Kay, Ken, and Steph. Ira comes in early and works in the classroom rather than gossiping in the copy room. Ira is the one who will discuss student achievement at the grade-level meeting, instead of discussing the Christmas party at the meeting. Ira is the one from whom you learn something every time you meet. He might be a thirty-year veteran or a third-year rookie. Here is the tricky part: because Ira is so reflective about practice, it is likely that he won't even realize he's an "Ira." He is always growing and improving and, therefore, humble. You might even be the one to tell Ira that he's an "Ira!"

 SCOOP

At this point, it might be tempting to categorize our colleagues as Kens, Iras, Stephs, or Kays, but we won't. People are much more complicated than the short caricatures we have created here. The truth is, if we look closely, we would see a bit of Ken, Kay, and Ira in all of us.

Your Parents

Getting to know the parents of your students is as important as getting to know your colleagues. Your biggest mistake would be to think of all of the following parent-contact tips and tools as low priorities and not your real job. At times, teachers, administrators, board members, and support staff lose sight of who really owns the schools. First, and always, we must acknowledge that parents are our customers—our stockholders. They pay our salaries, are our ultimate evaluators, and can be our greatest partners or roadblocks in the day-to-day business of teaching their children.

Over the last few years, too many educators have hung a "Testing—Do Not Disturb" sign on the school's front door and chased parents from their buildings. This is ironic, since parents and educators want the same thing— maximum student achievement.

Develop an effective "bedside manner." Think about your favorite doctor. He or she not only has a great deal of expertise but also has a knack for setting you at ease and earning your confidence. It is the same with the parents who send you their children. You need to develop an honest rapport with parents, setting them at ease and enlisting their support to develop their child's strengths and remediate their weaknesses. Parents want teachers to care for their children and challenge those children to reach their potential. "Care" comes before "challenge" in the dictionary and in the best classrooms. Here's another way to put it: Will parents consider you a Kay, a Ken, or an Ira?

Introductory Phone Call

Calling parents a week before school starts might sound like something right out of an old television sitcom, but it could go a long way toward establishing the vital link between school and home. It can also take the pressure off children to be messengers between teachers and parents. Instead, a relationship can bloom among adults whose common interest is the child. A phone conversation can segue into other more substantive discussions about, say, recommended books parents might enjoy with their children.

 SCOOP

Make sure that you can pronounce the child's and family's name correctly before you call.

Consider mailing a postcard to the children. Many families don't have working phone numbers.

Draft a short conversation in which you introduce yourself and give parents a chance to ask questions. Ask about ways parents would like to be involved in the classroom and what their goals are for their child this year. Tell them your goals for their child, too.

This is a two-way conversation. Take notes as you talk with parents so that you'll be ready to use students' preferred names on the first day, and more. There will be much to learn about your new class, and having a record of this initial conversation will refresh your memory before classes begin.

Making certain that you recognize every opportunity to reinforce that parents' expertise is valued and required for success will go miles toward improving student achievement in your room.

Try to anticipate some of the questions parents might ask. Practice what you might say if, for example, the parent tells you that last year's teacher gave too much homework.

Try to answer these questions before you make your introductory calls:
- What are the students going to learn this year?
- How are the students going to be graded?
- What is included on the report card/progress report? Grades? Conduct? Teacher comments? Skills checklist? Work habits?
- What is the policy on late work?
- How are differences in learning accommodated?
- What is the discipline policy?
- Is my child performing on grade level?

- Is there a gifted program and, if so, how does my child get into it?
- How can my child get extra help?
- How can a parent help a child at home?

 SCOOP

Don't promise to do something and not follow through. A common mistake teachers make is creating plans and goals that are too overwhelming in practice. Making promises and not maintaining them causes problems with parent and colleague relationships.

Many parents have had bad experiences that they will want to share. Be very careful to listen, but do not feed into any bad-mouthing of colleagues or your school. If you contact a parent who is angry about something that occurred with the school last year or over the summer:

- Stay calm and listen
- Don't interrupt. Resist the temptation to jump into problem-solving mode. Wait until the parent is finished.
- Remember—if parents are telling you about a previous problem, they are hoping that it won't happen again.

Now you have data about what they expect from you.

Some teachers go even further to reach out to their students before the first day of school and actually visit them at home. Nancy Karpyk, a nationally recognized kindergarten teacher from Weirton, West Virginia, brings with her a painted shoebox. She shakes the box and asks the child to guess what might be inside, which sets the stage for a fun initial conversation. When the box is opened, it reveals a seashell for the child to keep, and Karpyk explains that the first topic of the year will be the ocean (Briggs 2007).

Communicating With Parents During the School Year

The "golden rule" in communicating with parents, in person or by phone throughout the school year, is to always mention something positive about the student first. Regardless of the problems a student causes, a call or conference should never end without parents hearing about something that you like about their child. More importantly—parents should leave knowing that you want their child to be successful.

When the information you provide to parents is balanced, they are more likely to listen and act on it. Dwell only on the negative and families may form the idea that you do not care for the child, that there is personal dislike for this child, or that you are generally not fair. The student and his or her family might discount your opinion, and you will lose crucial support in dealing with the child's classroom learning and behavior. (Think Ken!) Be overly complimentary of a student who is experiencing problems and families may find you insincere. (Think Kay!)

One way to obtain more parental assistance when you encounter problems with students is to contact parents when their child is successful. Use a phone call or note to parents when there is good news to share. Some teachers allow students to make an occasional "brag call" to their parents when they reach a milestone or exceed expectations. Daily and weekly contacts are also examples of regular communication. One of our favorite principals, Susan Wells, has a Mickey Mouse phone in her office and has children call their parents to tell them of their successes. Another principal sends a postcard to the home with a celebration or "brag." Kids love getting mail. It makes them feel as important as you believe them to be.

Regardless of the topic, keep a record of your communications with parents. Phone calls can be challenging to track, particularly when they occur unexpectedly. You'll need a handy form that includes spaces for the date, time, child's name, and parents' names; the topic discussed; and notes. Use a tracking system that fits your organizational style. It's important to keep records to make sure that you're contacting all parents and not just a few. The records are for you, so keep them in a way that makes sense to you. See Appendix A for an example of a communication log. Adapt it to fit your needs.

 SCOOP

Parents complain that they were not made aware of their child's poor grades or failure to complete homework assignments until it was too late and the failing grades were in permanent ink on the report card. Your job is to enable parents to be your informed partners in the education of their son or daughter. Remember—short-cycle updates for parents are as important as short-cycle student assessments!

Classroom Newsletters

Classroom newsletters are powerful tools to reach parents and make them feel like a part of what is happening at school. Newsletters are also a means of gaining parents' support for the activities going on in the classroom. Newsletters reflect teachers and students, so they differ in format and style.

It is absolutely essential that you set a pattern for delivering the newsletter to parents and commit to it. If newsletters come home in backpacks at random, they will not be read consistently. From the start of the school year, let parents know when to expect the newsletters to arrive, and deliver them as promised.

Some schools designate one day per week to send all classroom newsletters and school communications to the home, inside a weekly folder. The folders also contain approaching homework assignments, and completed and graded work. Because everything of importance is consistently sent home in the folder on this day, parents know to look for it and to examine its contents.

Should homework be a part of your classroom newsletter? Many teachers do include upcoming homework assignments, or at least future project dates, in their newsletters. Other teachers put homework on a separate page that goes with the newsletter. Either format works. Tying the distribution of the newsletter and homework together increases the chance that both will receive proper attention at home.

SCOOP

Many parents admit that they don't know how to help their children. Use your newsletter to communicate topics of study and specific ways to support student learning.

Your newsletter is also a golden opportunity to show off the work and accomplishments of your class. Students could include their artwork, or articles and poetry they have written, or photos of classroom events. If you have had a recent visitor to the classroom, have your students publish an interview with this person in the newsletter.

In addition to student work and homework, newsletters may include:
- Important upcoming events in the classroom and school.
- Dates to remember.

- Curriculum notes and current topics of study.

- Materials needed in the classroom, or a wish list.

- Changes to class rules or policies.

- Details about field trips.

- Informational surveys.

- Messages of thanks for materials, or to volunteers.

- Ideas to help parents support kids at home.

- Ways for parents to be involved. (Parents have varying degrees of comfort in helping their students. Offer easy and concrete ways in which parents can support student success through everyday activities.)

- Photos of recent activities.

- Congratulations to students for achievements.

- Requests for volunteer support—remember to include ways for working parents to help you. Are there donated items that you need, like scrap paper? Discarded binders? Baby food jars? Parents who support your classroom will be more invested in the collective success of your classroom. Make all parents feel as if they have something to offer your class that will be beneficial to student outcomes.

You'll find many examples of class newsletters on the Web. Document templates may be downloaded from sources such as http://www.education-world.com/tools_templates/index.shtml (Education World) and http://office.microsoft.com/en-us/templates/default.aspx (Microsoft Office Online).

If many of your students' parents have Internet access through home or work, an e-mail newsletter or a classroom blog may be an even more efficient and effective way to reach them. Some teachers, like http://www.misterkindergarten.com/ ("Mr. Kindergarten" Dwayne Kohn), send short daily updates via e-mail, and include class activities, homework, congratulations, needed items, and a calendar of events. Kohn even shares a sample of his newsletter on his Web site. E-mail is a reliable, direct line to parents, and this method is faster, cheaper, and more environmentally friendly. It is also a simple task to print e-mail notes for parents who aren't currently on-line.

Newsletters are not only for kindergarten. They are appropriate for all elementary grades and, at times, beyond. In fact, one of the things we have learned over the years is that many "elementary" activities are very effective with middle school and high school students. Parents know that children can be tight lipped when it comes to sharing tidbits about the school day, and classroom newsletters fill in the gaps. Don't neglect to give parents a "conversation starter" in your newsletters, such as, "Ask your child about Tuesday's floating egg experiment."

Involving Parents with Homework

Homework is more than a means of review. It is also a means of communicating with parents and getting them involved in their child's learning. Interviews, family history activities, and even "create your own homework" assignments can stimulate discussion and get kids to open up about school.

Kelly Anderson gives the parents of her seventh and eighth grade students at R.B. Stewart Middle School in Zephyrhills, Florida, a unique homework assignment during the first week of school. She gives the students pages with the words: *Dazzling Dawg Request—In 1,000,000 Words Or Less, Please Tell Us About Your Child*. "Almost all of the parents took the request seriously and told me in this assignment more than I could possibly have learned while I have their children," reported Anderson (Bafile 2003).

There are many other ways to encourage parents to join their kids in assignments. When your class studies the importance of recycling, for example, you might have students log their recycling practices at home and look for additional paths to saving energy. Giving students a weekly assignment that requires reading to or interviewing a parent is another direct way to invite families to be more active participants in the educational process.

Are you intrigued by the traveling classroom stuffed "pets" that many students "adopt" for a day or a weekend at a time? In a twist on the popular *Flat Stanley* activities inspired by the Jeff Brown book, Ballentine Elementary sends an adorable bear named BES to *work*. Parents at the school sign up to have BES as a sidekick for a day of work. He has been to college, ridden in a fire truck, and rested on the anchor's desk during the news. Parents write about BES's day with them and return the bear with notes and photos from his day, and all of this information is posted at the Columbia (South Carolina) school. This homework assignment for parents encourages their involvement, while introducing students to the real tasks and responsibilities associated with many different careers. (Bafile 2007).

Parents Playing an Active Role

Members of students' families and other "dignitaries" visit Vicky Moore's second grade classroom in Temecula, California. About every three weeks, she figuratively and literally rolls out the red carpet for "Mystery Readers" who join the students and read a favorite story. The students guess the identities of the readers beforehand, through five clues that move from general to specific. Moore lines up the visitors early in the school year through e-mail contacts, etc. "As clues get more specific, I see their [the students'] eyes light up as they think—'Hey, I think that's my grandpa. He likes tennis and he has a pug.'" says Moore. When their brand-new principal served as the first Mystery Reader of the year, the students expected the custodian, until the last clue mentioned wearing a tie to school! (Bafile 2008).

Here are some suggestions to get parents involved:

- Invite them to attend class plays, presentations, poetry readings, etc.
- Make them a part of planning field trips, classroom celebrations, and other events.
- Tell them how they can help their children succeed in your class by reviewing for tests, proofreading homework, and more, without doing this work for the children.
- Ask parents about interests and expertise they have that they might be willing to share with the group.
- Be a resource by sharing information about child development, discipline, and other parenting topics, when it is appropriate.
- Periodically survey parents about how things are going.

Journal Activity

- *Write a sample script for an introductory phone conversation and your introductory letter that you might use with the parents of your new students. Have a colleague (or two) in your school read and critique your content and language choices. Choose somebody who has good data about your community, parents, students, and school. These people can help you learn about the culture of your students and their families.*

Your Students

You can take some comfort knowing that the first day of school is like a blind date for everyone. Even with their years of experience, veteran teachers are just like you, coming to a new school. No one, not a teacher or a student, returns to the same school they left last year. Mr. Harms might be a twenty-eight-year veteran of seventh grade math. Congratulations! But this year there's a new assistant principal, a new seventh grade book, or a new schedule. Maybe Mr. Harms gets the Rempala twins this year, two boys who think "No Child Left Behind" means that they should annoy *everyone.*

What's your first order of business? Put aside teaching standard 4.01 for a moment. Instead, concentrate on getting to know your students, students getting to know each other, and students getting to know themselves. The time spent collecting this data will pay big dividends throughout the year.

The more you know about your students' background knowledge, interests, culture, and learning styles, the better your relationships, classroom management, and instruction will be. Just how critical is this information? Robert Marzano, one of the foremost educational researchers, believes that "the quality of relationships teachers have with students is the keystone of effective management and perhaps even the entirety of teaching." (Marzano 2007).

Find a colleague who can take you on a tour of the community where your students live. Do your students live in single-family homes or apartments? Are they walkers or bus riders? Are there recreational facilities for use after school and during the summer months? See what businesses are located in the district.

In some communities, things can change quickly. So even if you think you know the neighborhood from working there last year, check again. Often these driving tours are revelations. You will see the poor conditions in which many students live, revealing why schoolwork may not be the first thing on their minds. After you have developed a relationship with one of your parents, have that parent give you a community tour, too. He or she may provide a very different perspective than a colleague.

SCOOP

Be careful to recognize biases that you have, based on what you observe. Recognizing your biases will help you keep them from invading your speech and actions when building your relationships.

Interests

Beg, borrow, or build a questionnaire and an interview script for use during the first week of school. Both your questionnaire and interview should elicit a variety of data to confirm the basic information you have about where students live, etc., and help you form a more complete picture of each student. Ask students how they learn best. Asking them to write and talk about themselves and their learning can provide you and them with valuable data.

They may share information about siblings and extended family members who might live with them. You can learn how they spend their time outside of school. For example, are they supervised, or left to their own resources? Are they on a soccer or basketball team? Are they in a Brownie troop? Do they work at a fast-food restaurant? The survey can even reveal how they interact with and view other members of the class. You also want to learn what your students value. Asking questions about whom and what they admire can give you insight into their cultural norms.

Use an interest survey several times during the school year, as well as other methods to elicit student data. Don't pass out the #2 pencils on the first day of school, require students to use their best handwriting, and quietly complete survey questions. If you want to know what makes your students tick, you're going to have to be more creative than that.

Getting to know your students is important, regardless of your grade level. If you're teaching primary grades, consider giving each student a small journal and some old magazines and see what they value. They can paste pictures of their interests and date that page. They can add to the journal as their interests grow and evolve throughout the year. Have them interview one another and introduce themselves to you. If you're in a secondary classroom, have students bring in pictures of people who are important to them. Have them write poetry or songs. And, perhaps most importantly, model the activity by participating along with your students. Students who know and love their teacher will work harder to meet their expectations.

A student's passion for the Dallas Cowboys can quickly move to NASCAR. The fascination with a specific toy or classmate can quickly become indifference. This is why we suggest spending a few minutes every day with students, talking about their interests and life inside and outside of school. Kay Serra has the right idea. She just overdoes it, spending half the morning chatting with students. You will be amazed at the wealth of unconventional and valuable information you can gain from brief "morning meetings." Purposeful collection of student interests doesn't just help you to form relationships, it helps you to develop engaging units and assessments.

Morning meetings also offer students choices when it comes to the way they communicate their interests, talents, and home life. Students who might struggle to write about these things will often be able to talk passionately about them, draw them, or describe them to you in a one-on-one conversation. These meetings also allow students to learn about their classmates as the discussion unfolds. If you work in a neighborhood school, morning meetings may be a critical time for students to begin to collectively make sense of neighborhood drama before they can become ready to learn that day.

Second-grade teacher Kathy Gaji of Brookside Elementary School in Binghamton, New York, has a check-in that is part her class's daily morning routine. This quick meeting allows her to connect with her students in a personal way every day. "I sit at my desk with an alphabetized checklist of names in front of me," she explains. "As the children bring their bags of books and pencils to me, I greet them and check off their names. This is a good time for a quick word of encouragement, a reminder of needing to turn in late homework, or just a quick hello. It helps me connect with the kids as individuals, rather than just as members of my class" (Bafile 2006).

Learning Styles

Walk into Ira Flect's classroom on a typical day, and you have to be careful not to interrupt a group of students in the corner, writing rap lyrics to explain the difference between a fruit and a vegetable; disturb another group who is creating a survey at the computer center to determine and graph the students' favorite lunch item; or step on the "What Should I Eat?" game, in which the students describe the nutritional value of various food.

In Ira's classroom, children can choose from a variety of media and methods to learn. Songs and games are as legitimate a way to learn as writing and doing science experiments. Ira believes that *how* children learn is as important as *what* they learn, and the best learning happens when the activity fits the student's learning style. Ira has used the data collected from his students and their parents to improve student engagement.

It may feel overwhelming to consider how you might cater to every student's interests, cultural background, natural intelligence, or learning style. Take small steps and think about choices. Involve students in the design of assessments, and they will tell you how they would best like to show you what they know. Understanding how students best communicate their learning to you can help you better deliver instruction that hits the mark for more students. There are several inventories you can use with your students to explore ways that they might learn best. Exhibit 1, developed by Laura Candler, is one of our favorites.

Academics

Review student cumulative records to gather data about your students as learners. Analyze state test data to identify strengths and weaknesses in individual students and the class as a whole. Ask to see a copy of your school's state report card and find out if your state offers on-line reports, such as item analyses and individual student reports.

 SCOOP

Be careful when reading teacher comments in cumulative folders or listening to subjective commentary from other teachers. Ken Tankerous is quick to develop preconceived notions about students that affect the way he treats them, while Kay Serra believes that every child deserves a clean slate each year.

Ira doesn't discount the important information he finds in teacher comments that is critical to vertical communication between grade level and student success. Giving kids a clean slate is not in their best interest when it comes to support and intervention.

As a classroom teacher, you need to know if there are students in your class who have an individualized educational plan (IEP) in place. If so, review the plan to determine how special services will be delivered. Will the student report to a resource room for part of the day, or will the special-education teacher be with you in your room? Having another professional in your room will be very helpful to you, but will require planning and coordination.

Make an appointment with the special-education teacher in your building to review the IEP goals of your students and discuss how you will work together to help them achieve these goals. Special-education law requires all students to master the grade-level state standards. This can best be done in your room, with support. The sooner you develop an ownership for students with disabilities, the better off they will be. Take responsibility for the success of *all* of your students.

 SCOOP

Most schools and parents work hard for special-needs students to be included in the regular classroom. There is a continuum of student needs in your room, and you must provide a continuum of support. When you believe that all students have a right to learn in your classroom and that you have a responsibility to make that happen, labels (and the stigma attached) cease to matter. "John is a student with a learning disability" will carry the same weight as "John is an Aries" or "Emma is a Virgo."

EXHIBIT 1

How Many Ways Are *You* Smart

Directions: Fold the paper vertically on the dark line so that the columns with the eight "multiple intelligences" are hidden. Read each statement below. Place a check next to each item that is true about you. Then unfold the paper and circle the X in each row that you marked. Write the total number of X's in each column at the bottom of the paper. How many ways are you smart?

Which of the following are true about you?

	Nature Smart	Number/Logic Smart	Word Smart	Music Smart	Picture Smart	Body Smart	People Smart	Self Smart
I enjoy singing and I sing fairly well.				X				
I enjoy crossword puzzles and word games.			X					
I'm good at solving jigsaw puzzles.					X			
I can read maps easily.					X			
I learn best when I can talk over a new idea.							X	
Picture, line, and bar graphs are easy to understand.					X			
I like to listen to music in my free time.				X				
I get along well with different types of people.							X	
I like writing about my thoughts and feelings.								X
Protecting the environment is very important to me.	X							
I enjoy caring for pets and other animals.	X							
I like drama and acting things out.						X		
I'm good at writing stories.			X					
I can understand difficult math ideas easily.		X						
I play a musical instrument (or would like to).				X				
People tell me I'm good at sports or dancing.						X		
I'm good at figuring out patterns.		X						
My best way to learn is by doing hands-on activities.						X		
I like spending time by myself.								X
I find that I'm often helping other people.							X	
I'm naturally good at taking care of plants.	X							
I enjoy solving problems and "brainteasers."		X						
Having quiet time to think over ideas is important to me.								X
I enjoy reading for pleasure.			X					
TOTALS								

"MULTIPLE INTELLIGENCES"

Developed by Laura Candler (Teaching Resources at www.lauracandler.com)

Journal Activity

• *Take out your calendar and make your year-long plan for collecting student-interest data.*

The Plan

Putting Your Data to Work

Whether the data is from a cumulative folder, a phone conversation with a parent, an interest survey, or a morning meeting, isn't as important as what *happens* to the information after you have it. The essence of being an extraordinary teacher is using this data—this information—to adapt your interactions, instruction, and assessments (Reeves 2008b). Ira knows that the real power of data is unleashed only if it impacts the way you teach.

 SCOOP

If you are not going to do something with information, then don't ask for it!

Journal Activity

• *What do you know about your students, parents, and colleagues? Create your list from the data you have collected. In Exhibit 2, the left column shows some data that Ira Flect might choose to list. The column on the right is for you to create your own list.*

EXHIBIT 2	
Creating Your List from Data You Have Collected	
Ira's List	**Your List**

STUDENTS:
- High poverty, large Appalachian population
- Mostly strategic and intensive on fall benchmarks on the Dynamic Indicators of Basic Early Literacy Skills (DIBELS)
- Lots of boys, sports are big—soccer!!
- Lack of male role models

PARENTS:
- Few working phone numbers
- Distrustful of school
- High rate of illiteracy
- Many single-parent homes

COLLEAGUES:
- Districtwide push for integrating reading across the content areas
- DIBELS is a single data point used to make big decisions for student interventions
- Many opportunities for intervention and support of struggling readers
- Little to no sharing of instructional successes between teachers

Not familiar with DIBELS? See Appendix B.

Reflect on what you know about your students, their community, and their parents. Now, develop some big goals for the school year. Our rule of thumb is that you should be able to write all of these goals on your hand—excuse the pun! In other words, don't create thirty or twenty or even ten goals. Try to develop five.

Make a list of the things you want to accomplish this year, over a cup of coffee. Be careful. Your first draft will probably be a mix of big goals (increase reading levels, reduce the number of bus referrals) and little goals (get carpet squares for reading groups, download state practice tests, etc.).

Most plans fail when the big goals get pushed aside by the little goals. Why? Big goals, such as improving reading or behavior, are critical, but they do not necessarily have a completion date tied to them. But little goals, such as getting carpet squares, responding to an e-mail, or returning a phone call, are time-dependent even if they're not very important. Therefore, school days and school years become a long series of little goals. As a result, even if you've managed to check off everything from your "to do" list, at the end of the day, or at the end of the year, you often tell yourself, "I'm exhausted, but I don't think I really accomplished anything."

Here are suggestions for making sure that your goals are big and "SMART."

Specific—   Your big goals should be straightforward and specific, and they should emphasize what you want to happen. Instead of setting a goal to have your students' reading levels improve, set a specific goal to improve their DIBELS scores by 25 percent, or create a goal for a certain AYP subgroup.

Measurable—   If you can't measure your big goal, you can't manage it. Build in short-term and long-term measurements. The short-term measurements can provide encouragement or serve as a warning sign that things are not working.

Attainable—   Attainable means "doable" but is not a synonym for "easy." Be sure to set big goals that you and you students can attain with some effort! When goals are too difficult, you set the stage for failure. However, goals that are too low send the message that you aren't trying. And remember, if the goals are too easy or are the same for all students, achievement gaps between student groups will never be closed.

Relevant—   Your big goals should represent things over which you have immediate and direct control. Establishing a goal for your students to get a good night's sleep is admirable, but are you going to be there to tuck them in?

Timely—   Set a time frame for your big goals, such as "by the end of the first month" or "by the end of the first quarter." If you don't set a time, or set a time that is too far off, the commitment is too vague. It tends not to happen because you feel you can start working on it next week, or the week after that. Without a time limit, there's no urgency to start. Putting checkpoints on your goal gives you a clear target. Also, don't forget the other "T"—*tracking*. Keep careful records of your progress toward your big goals. When you're feeling down about where you and your students are in the third week of November, it's great to be able to look back and see how far everyone has come since September!

Two examples of big SMART goals, one academic and the other behavioral, are presented in Exhibit 3.

SMART goals are important, and the two examples in Exhibit 3 were easy to write. These two goals are certainly big and SMART. They may be similar to the goals your principal might develop with you at a staff meeting or at your post-evaluation conference. Certainly no one can argue with the importance of increasing reading fluency or instructional time. We could end the chapter here, but we know the truth. Big SMART goals are not enough!

Here's the million-dollar question: Once you close your classroom door and you're alone with your students, just what are you going to do to accomplish these goals? Most SMART goals look great on paper, but they are only as good as the instruction we provide . . . and that's the scary part. You look around the staff meeting and you imagine that all of your colleagues know exactly how to engage and accelerate the learning of that third-grader who is only reading twenty-eight words per minute in the fall, when the benchmark is fifty-three words per minute. The quiet smile on their faces as they nod at their principal's request confirms your worst fear: you alone possess the illiterate, out-of-control classroom and have no idea how to deal with it.

Here's the truth. Yes, there are veteran colleagues in your midst who have found success in accelerating student achievement and classroom management. However, many of your colleagues face each group of children and their set of SMART goals with the same fear and confusion that you feel.

Ira uses his data not just to develop his big SMART goals, but also to decide what he will need to do to accomplish his goals. He will identify those things that can help him, and roadblocks that may stand in his way. The following information on "SMART Goals" presents a template suggesting how you can organize your data to better plan how to accomplish your big SMART goals. You'll probably have better ideas, and we encourage you to use them. Our template is simply intended as a way to get you started.

EXHIBIT 3
Two Examples of Big SMART Goals

Academic Goal

S   Specific   Increase students' reading fluency.

M   Measurable   Using DIBELS progress-monitoring probes, student progress will be charted and tracked.

A   Attainable   Students will increase their instructional recommendation—intensive to strategic and strategic to benchmark.

R   Relevant   I will progress-monitor the intensive students weekly, and the strategic students two times a month.

T   Timely   Students' success will be measured at the winter benchmark data collection.

(For more information on DIBELS assessments for monitoring student reading fluency, visit www.dibels.uoregon.edu.)

Behavioral Goal

S   Specific   I will increase the amount of instructional time during my day by reducing the time spent in transition.

M   Measurable   Students will be timed during transitions and the times will be graphed on a poster displayed in the classroom.

A   Attainable   Students will reduce the time spent in transition by 60 percent.

R   Relevant   I will chart transition time between activities, like movement between centers, restroom breaks, and morning work, daily.

T   Timely   The increased instructional time will be displayed weekly outside the classroom and shared with the principal monthly, for incentive.

(For other examples of ways to chart student behavior, see www.interventioncentral.com.)

SMARTI Goals

We're suggesting that you add an "I" to your SMART goals. The "I" in SMARTI is what "I know," what "I think," and then, most importantly, what "I do." We've created a template (Exhibit 4) to help you organize these ideas.

What do you know? What information have you gathered about your students, parents, and community as it relates to your goal? What are the norms of your school? What do you know about your colleagues?

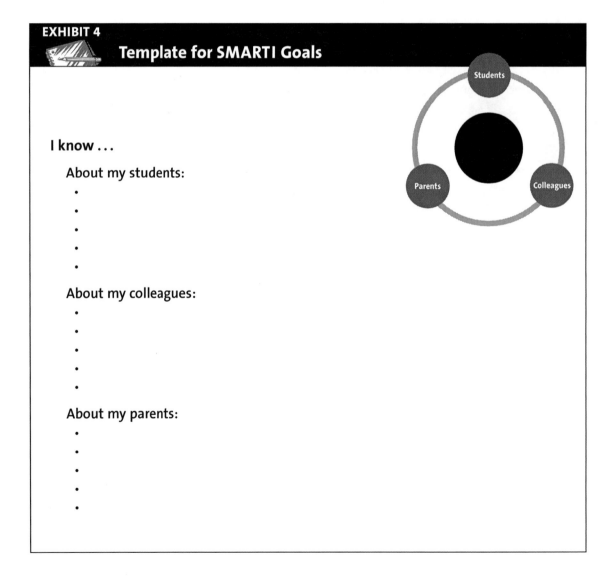

EXHIBIT 4

Template for SMARTI Goals

I know . . .

   About my students:
-
-
-
-
-

   About my colleagues:
-
-
-
-
-

   About my parents:
-
-
-
-
-

Take the information you gathered for your earlier journal activity and place it in the template (Exhibit 4).

Ira Flect's completed template is shown in Exhibit 5.

Next, Ira used the data to uncover roadblocks and support for his big SMARTI goal—Improving Reading Fluency.

This is the messy part. We've discovered that the hardest work is often the messy part! Ira uses what he knows to form hypotheses, generate ideas—even crazy ones—and think about what he knows

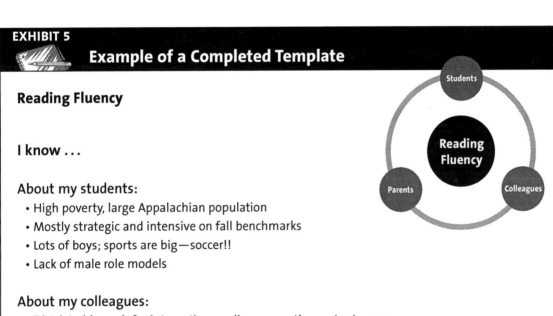

EXHIBIT 5

Example of a Completed Template

Reading Fluency

I know . . .

About my students:
- High poverty, large Appalachian population
- Mostly strategic and intensive on fall benchmarks
- Lots of boys; sports are big—soccer!!
- Lack of male role models

About my colleagues:
- Districtwide push for integrating reading across the content areas
- DIBELS is a single data point used to make big decisions for student interventions
- Many opportunities for intervention and support of struggling readers
- Little to no sharing of instructional successes between teachers

About my parents:
- Few working phone numbers
- High rate of illiteracy
- Distrustful of school
- Many single-parent homes

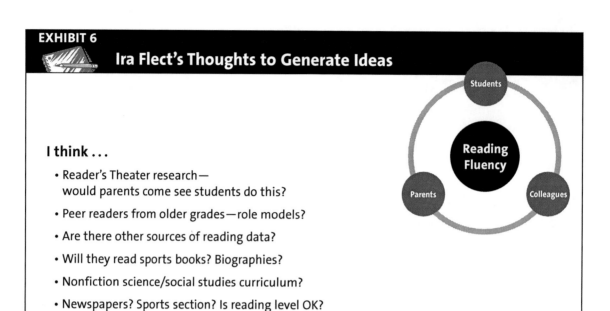

that could support or block his reading goal for students. Exhibit 6 lists some things that we heard Ira say when he was thinking.

Remember—sometimes your best thinking is a stream of consciousness. It's not neat and organized. Try to write down all of your ideas about how your data will influence your goal.

Next, Ira crafts his "I need to do" statements. "I do" statements come from analyzing what you know about your current situation and thinking about ways to achieve your goal. Ira Flect's data indicates that his students have few male role models and that many of his students come from single-family homes. Asking Mom to read with her kids every night is going to be a tough sell. Ira sees the need to hook students up with reading role models to practice reading fluently.

EXHIBIT 7

Ira Flect's "I Do" Process

I do . . .

- Talk to sixth-grade teachers about having reading buddies weekly on Wednesday morning following music class.

- Identify pieces of real writing in periodicals for students who are on or below grade level for student fluency practice. Seek real-world examples of current writing about content standards to share with students.

- Progress-monitor reading fluency, but also:
  - Conduct running records on all students, to better understand student miscues.
  - Assess reading comprehension monthly, using the building's common assessments of reading program materials.
  - Use the data to determine my grouping of students for intervention.

- Work to educate my parents. Put a reading research fact in each newsletter and explain what kids are doing in class that demonstrates it.

- Have students perform one of their reader's theater pieces as an evening event. Use my PTA money to help buy pizza to serve. Use the time to teach parents some strategies to support their readers at home, like why it's good practice for students to practice "easy" text and what kinds of "thinking" questions they could ask their students about the text.

(Diagram: Central circle labeled "Reading Fluency" surrounded by Students, Colleagues, Parents)

Ira also knows that his boy-dominant classroom is very sports-minded. His students read what they are interested in. In addition, Ira sees an opportunity to work on topics that are in the third-grade science and social studies curriculum.

Ira realizes, too, that his school offers many supports for students who are not performing at the DIBELS benchmark, but there is more to his readers than a fluency score. And, he knows that his parents are distrustful of school. In some instances, interventions are being denied students because parents don't want their child in a "special" class.

He then makes some decisions based on all of this information. Ira's "I do" process is shown in Exhibit 7.

Now, it is time for you to complete a template for one of *your* big SMARTI goals. Go to Exhibit 8 and fill in all you can about what you know, what you think, and what you can do.

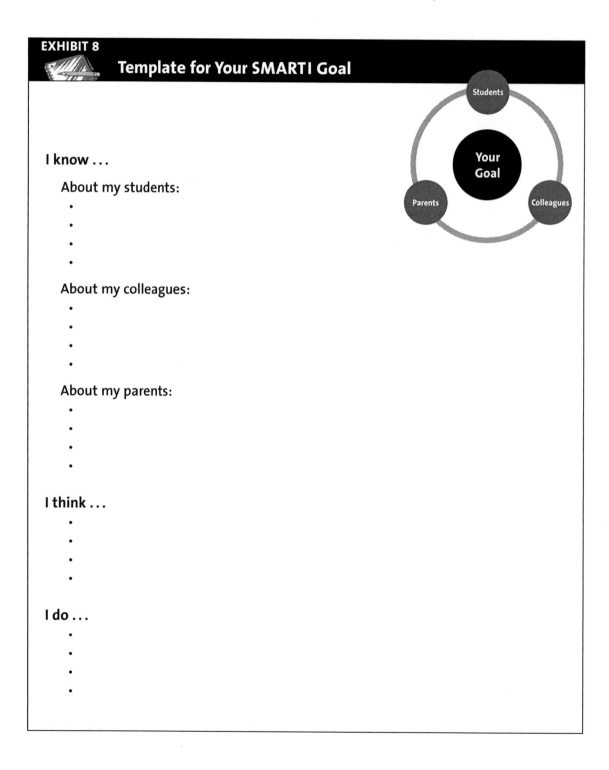

EXHIBIT 8

Template for Your SMARTI Goal

I know . . .

    About my students:
-
-
-
-

    About my colleagues:
-
-
-
-

    About my parents:
-
-
-
-

I think . . .
-
-
-
-

I do . . .
-
-
-

High Expectations

There will be a day, and likely several, when you will think that teaching standard A03.9 is going to be impossible. You'll fantasize about alternate career opportunities in hotel/motel management and ask yourself, *Can I really make a difference? Are these kids ever going to get it?* The Kens in your building will say, "No!"

Perhaps many of your students come from poor and sometimes difficult homes. They speak a different language or have an IEP. Is it fair to have high expectations of yourself and of them? Would it be wrong to have compassion for their circumstances and give yourself and these students a break? The Kays in your building will say, "No!"

Teachers, and at times entire school districts, can get caught up in the thesis that certain children can't achieve at high levels. They spend endless hours excusing, tracking, and correlating the percentage of low-birth weight babies, percent of children born to single moms, percent of children from families who receive government assistance, and the percentage of children with disabilities. Armed with printouts, statistics, and newspaper clippings, they will lament that, "We are not strong enough to raise poor, ethnic minority, or disabled students to a higher level, due to forces outside the school tugging them downward." And then these teachers start settling for "good enough" work. As a result, schools don't expect very much from themselves or their students—and in turn they don't get much from either group.

You don't have to look hard to find research supporting the notion that some children are destined to fail. In 1966, Professor James S. Coleman published a congressionally mandated study on why school-children in minority neighborhoods performed at far lower levels than children in suburban areas. Titled "Equality of Educational Opportunity," his mammoth, 737-page study reached the unsettling conclusions that teachers and schools were not society's great equalizers after all, and that the main cause of the achievement gap was in the backgrounds and resources of families (Coleman *et al.* 1966).

More than forty years later, some researchers still argue that we cannot count on schools to close gaps. They'll cite dozens of reasons why schools and teachers are doomed to come up short. A lack of affordable housing makes poorer children more transient and, therefore, more prone to switching schools midyear and losing progress. Higher rates of lead poisoning, asthma, and inadequate pediatric care also fuel low achievement, along with something as basic as the lack of eyeglasses. Even the way middle- and lower-class parents talk and read to their children is different, making learning more fun and creative for wealthier children.

"The Family: America's Smallest School Report," developed by Educational Testing Service (Barton and Coley 2007), recently examined the family and home experiences that influence children's learning. Their conclusion: "Our analysis shows that factors like single-parent families, parents reading to children, hours spent watching television and school absences, when combined, account for about two-thirds of the large differences among states in National Assessment of Educational Progress (NAEP) reading scores."

For many educators and policy makers, research like the Coleman Report and the very recent ETS study raises a haunting question: Do outside forces tug so hard that they cannot be overcome by any particular kind of school, any set of in-school reforms, or an effective and caring teacher? What if schools and teachers are not the answer?

Before throwing your hands up and exclaiming, "There's nothing I can do," the other side of this debate deserves consideration. Evidence based on different data and analytic methods attests to the success of teachers and schools in "beating the odds" and producing well-educated youngsters in spite of the hostile forces at work in many of their kids' lives.

Doug Reeves's case study on 90/90/90 schools (2004; 90/90/90 chapter available for free download at www.LeadandLearn.com) is "must" reading. This inspiring study focuses on 90/90/90 schools, in which 90 percent of the students were members of ethnic minorities, 90 percent of the students were eligible for free or reduced lunch, and 90 percent met or exceeded state academic standards.

Reeves found five characteristics that were common to all 90/90/90 schools.
   • A focus on academic achievement.
   • Clear curriculum choices.
   • Frequent assessment of student progress and multiple opportunities for improvement.
   • An emphasis on nonfiction writing.
   • Collaborative scoring of student work.

Today, Reeves is energizing educators with reports of "100-100-100" schools. Also, read Haycock *et al.*'s (1998) excellent publication, "Dispelling the Myth" (available for download at www.edtrust.org).

High-performing and high-poverty schools are not simply urban legends. They do exist. Here are some real examples we recently came across as we worked with the Houston Independent School District (HISD).

The HISD is the largest public school system in Texas, and the seventh largest in the United States. HISD is working hard to become Houstonians' K-12 school system of choice by constantly improving instruction and management to be as effective, productive, and economical as possible. We were working with this district developing school improvement plans. We didn't go there looking for high-performing, high-poverty schools, but they were there, just as they are all around the country.

Exhibit 9 lists HISD schools that have achieved 90 percent or higher on the 2007 math, reading, or writing segments of the 2007 Texas Assessment of Knowledge and Skills Test (TAKS) and have at least 90 percent of their students eligible for free or reduced lunches.

EXHIBIT 9

2007 Spring TAKS Passing Rate

2007 Spring TAKS Passing Rate
High Achieving/High Poverty
Houston Independent School District (HISD) Schools

90 Percent Poverty and 90 Percent Achievement on TAKS Reading	90 Percent Poverty and 90 Percent Achievement on TAKS Math	90 Percent Poverty and 90 Percent Achievement on TAKS Writing
Codwell Elementary	Allen Elementary	Allen Elementary
Excellence Middle	Burrus Elementary	Barrick Elementary
J.P. Henderson Elementary	De Zavala Elementary	Bellfort Academy
Kaleidoscope Middle	Excellence Middle	Benbrook Elementary
Kennedy Elementary	Herrera Elementary	Berry Elementary
Montgomery Elementary	J.P. Henderson Elementary	Bowie Elementary
Ross Elementary	Kennedy Elementary	Cage Elementary
Scott Elementary	McDade Elementary	Carrillo Elementary
White Elementary	Montgomery Elementary	Coop Elementary
	Oates Elementary	Cunningham Elementary
	Seguin Elementary	Davila Elementary
	Sherman Elementary	Durkee Elementary
	White Elementary	Edison Middle
		Emerson Elementary
		Excellence Academy
		Excellence Middle
		Gregg Elementary
		Grissom Elementary
		Herrera Elementary
		J.P. Henderson Elementary
		Janowski Elementary
		Kaleidoscope Middle
		Key Middle
		Mading Elementary
		Montgomery Elementary
		Oates Elementary
		Rodriguez Elementary
		Ross Elementary
		Sinclair Elementary
		Southmayd Elementary
		Stevenson Middle
		Sugar Grove Elementary
		Sutton Elementary
		Wesley Elementary
		White Elementary
		Woodson Middle
		Young Scholars

Some might argue that our list is too short to mean very much—forty-five schools. But the fact is, it shows that it can be done. And really, if someone needs more than this example to prove that high-poverty and high-achievement schools are possible, they probably have a different agenda. The real work is not in proving the existence of these schools; it's in replicating their success in more schools.

Psychologically, we can think of few things more terrifying than choosing or staying in a profession that has no impact or chance of changing a student's life. We are teachers, not potted plants (Reeves 2004b). Students don't march past us year after year without having us touch their hearts and minds, and vice versa. Intuitively, you know this is true.

Mistake of the Heart

Kay Serra rejects the notion of high failure rates for poor students but makes a mistake of the heart. All of her students pass because she gives credit for attendance, or for being non-disruptive and polite. She'll give A's and B's for C—or worse, D—work. She'll inflate scores based on effort or on the lack of support at home. Kay will accept assignments from students any day of the year with any excuse. She may even excuse some subgroups from completing her assignments at all. Students don't fail Kay's assignments—it's society that fails her students. Her justification is usually: "She is trying so hard;" "He is much better behaved than his brother whom I had last year;" "This will be so good for her self-esteem;" "At home, he has to sleep on a couch;" or "She is hungry, tired, and her clothes are dirty when she comes to school in the morning."

All of these statements are heart wrenching. And who wouldn't want to give these students a break, especially those who are academically struggling? However, politeness and effort are not "literacy" or "math" skills. There's only one answer: these students cannot read, write, or solve a two-digit addition problem. We do not tolerate different schools, buses, or bathrooms for students based on socio-economics or ethnicity, so how can we tolerate variations in learning expectations or standards? A million-dollar industry has developed to make certain that educators understand the culture of poverty. But understanding often dissolves into pity, lowered expectations, and grade inflation.

Doug Reeves (2006) warns us that, despite what some teachers like Kay think, grade inflation is not a victimless crime. There's only one thing to call this practice—a lie. If we are truly worried about students, imagine how they feel when state tests, college registrars, or employees tell them they really don't have what it takes, despite being told by us that they were proficient or exemplary students.

Kay may think that she is "protecting" children by not telling the students and parents the truth. That truth is: *You are behind your classmates, and we will all have to work harder, longer, and smarter to catch you up. This will be hard work and require more effort than that of some of your classmates, so we will have to help each other along the way. But catching up is so important that we have to do whatever it takes* (Reeves, 2006)*!*

The reality is that nearly all students will be tested on the grade-level standards at the end of the year. Teachers can complain that this is unfair, but it is not unfair, it is hard—hard for students, hard for parents, and hard for teachers. It is unfair, however, to let a student fall behind. We cannot accept poverty, disabilities, or language acquisition as an excuse for falling behind.

Mistake of the Head

Does Ken Tankerous have high expectations for all students? He sure does! He refuses to accept late or sloppy work, regardless of the quality of the content, all in the name of high expectations. He takes points away from disruptive or loud students, all in the name of high expectations. While his colleagues give an assignment and explain to students what proficient work should look like, Ken assigns "gotcha homework." With no scoring guide or sample of proficient work, his students have to guess what Ken's notion of proficient work looks like. Many guess wrong!

Ken will argue that responsibility is the primary skill demanded of all adults in the workforce and that it is his civic duty to require this level of compliance. When students fail Ken's assignment—the one he wrote in 1972—it's the students who fail. Sorting kids and having them imitate responsible grown-ups takes precedence over teaching kids.

It is likely that the achievement gaps we hear and read so much about will not be eliminated until we stop giving up on some students or giving up on ourselves and blaming it on bad habits and bad attitudes. Maybe a new law should be passed—No Grown-Up Left Behind. High expectations without high levels of effective support equals bad teaching. And, hiding behind offerings of ineffective support is malpractice. Ken says, "I told them they could e-mail me for help," but he knows that most students *will* not and some *can*not. Someone needs to point out his faulty logic. If year after year your interventions don't work, then they are not really interventions! Maybe it's time Ken checked out what they're doing in Houston with "those" kids.

Ira catches himself whenever he asks, "Are these kids ever going to get this?" He knows that it's more precise and useful to ask, "In my class, with my instruction, do these kids have a chance of getting it?" When students fail Ira's assignment—it's Ira who has failed—because he knows it can be done, and is being done, with and for the kids who need it most. Of course it would be easier if all of societies' social and health problems were erased, but it can be done anyway. It *is* being done.

Journal Activity

• Examine your class test data from last year and find students who performed below the proficient level on your state test. Now, examine the class grades you gave those students. You will probably find passing grades of A, B, or C. How do you explain the two different performance levels? Is there a gender or ethnicity pattern with these students? Reflect on what you discover about your practice and identify areas for your own growth.

• Now let's test your Ira Quotient (IQ) on a bigger idea—creating a high-expectation school. Your "to do" list is going to be about influencing your school's culture, in addition to that of your classroom. When it comes to high expectations, you should identify sources of support for your mission, and opportunities for entrée and influence outside your classroom. Exhibit 10 shows how Ira might look at things. Exhibit 11 is where you have your chance to develop ideas for creating a high-excpectaton school.

EXHIBIT 10
Ira's High Expectations

I know . . .

About my students:
- They believe that good behavior = good grades.
- They expect effort to be rewarded.

About my colleagues:
- Ruby Payne Study used to excuse students' behavior.
- Homework expectations are minimal.
- Good citizenship awards given, honor roll not given.

About my parents:
- Few parents have higher than a high school diploma, many without even that.

I think (Remember, this is messy!) . . .
- College is not a part of students' lives. College talk might upset parents who can't afford it.
- There is a grading issue in terms of separating behavior for learning and actual learning — rubric?
- Homework expectations need to increase. Parents angry? Need support.
- Should there be explicit talk with students about performance rubric?

I do . . .
- Have all staff wear college sweatshirts once a month to promote safe, happy college talk. Visit local campus in the spring.
- Create rubrics with students that evaluate learning behaviors separately from academic standards.
- Explicitly explain academic standards evaluation rubrics to students and parents before and after each assessment.
- Include homework assignments in weekly newsletter. Design specific support plans for all students who are unable or unwilling to complete assignments until homework expectations are met.

EXHIBIT 11

Your High Expectations

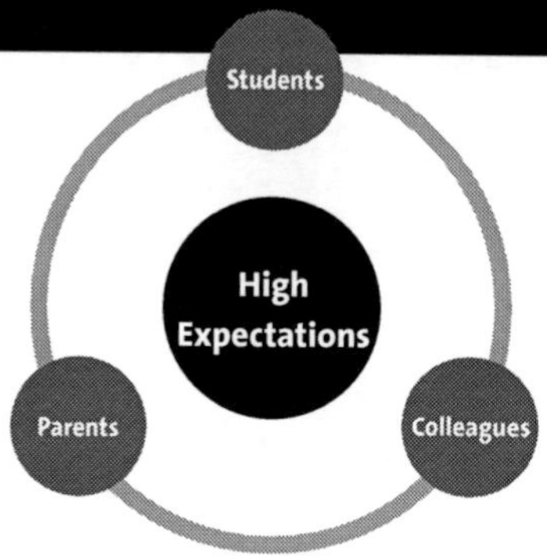

I know . . .

About my students:
-
-
-
-

About my colleagues:
-
-
-
-

About my parents:
-
-
-
-

I think (Remember, this is messy!) . . .
-
-
-
-
-
-

I do . . .
-
-
-
-
-

What Do You Mean I Only Have Two Days to Teach Double-Digit Addition?

How much time do you have to teach? Not much!

Consider a full-calendar year—365 days. Now, subtract summer vacation, which is about eighty-six days. Next, subtract weekends and holidays—about ninety-six more days. Let's not forget professional-development days, early dismissal, parent conferences, snow days, fog days, and "someone smelled gas" days. They eat up about twelve days. There are also class field trips, picnics, Thanksgiving parties, holiday wrapping day, Kwanza, Hanukkah, awards assembly, and concerts. Maybe that's another deduction of ten days. Oh, we almost forgot—you still have to deduct your state's testing days—that's ten more.

EXHIBIT 12

The Full-Year Calendar

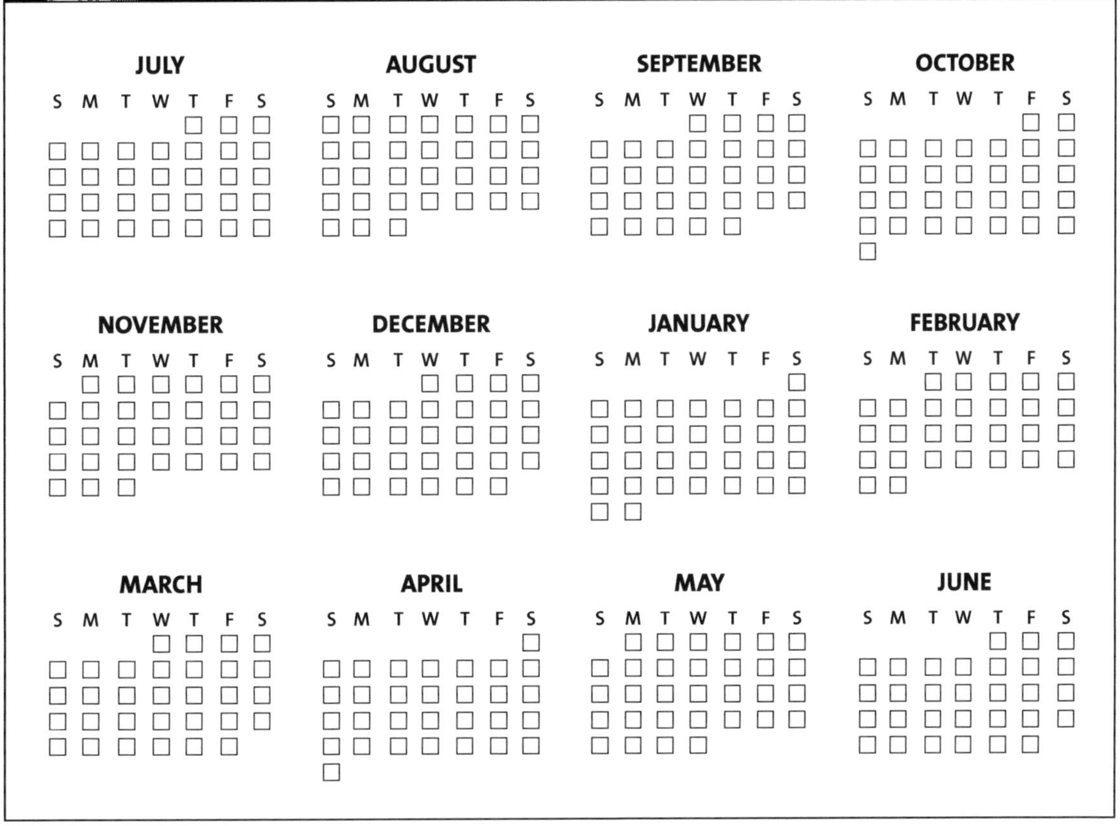

EXHIBIT 13

The Real Teaching Calendar: *What We Really Have*

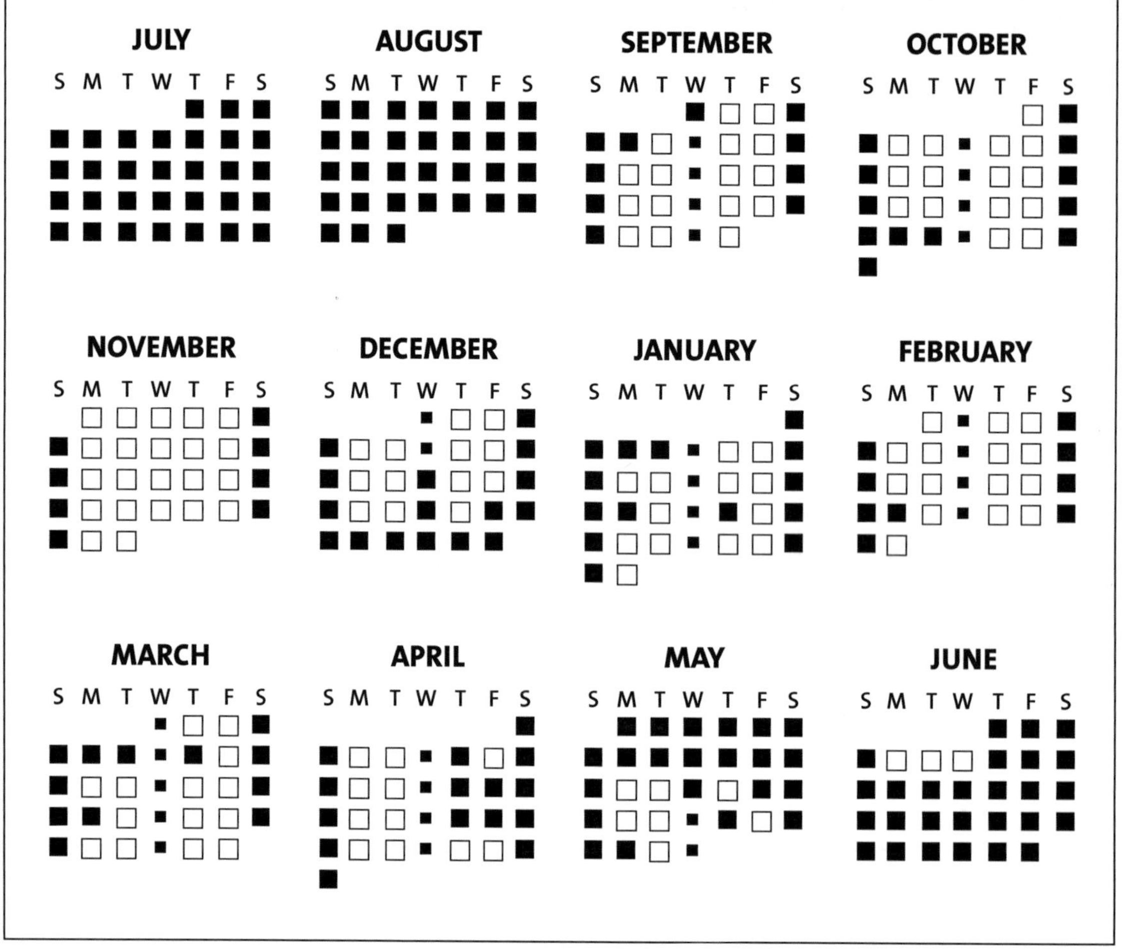

What starts out looking like gobs of time is quickly whittled down. You and your students are eventually left with about 150 days to teach and learn. Assuming you spend an hour a day on reading instruction, that equals about nineteen eight-hour days. Think how little you learned on your job the first nineteen days (Zattura Sims-El 2006).

The First Steps to Take

Once you realize the actual amount of time that you will have to teach, it becomes clear that you and your students can't afford to squander a minute. It is up to you to identify time-wasters—even small ones—and eliminate them. This list is different for every teacher, but it may include things like disorganization or lack of SMARTI goals, too much "chat time" with peers, poor classroom management, failure to take advantage of available technological tools, and more.

A Schedule

You will need a daily schedule that works, and one that is posted for everyone to see. You can alter a schedule, but first you must have one. Some things to put on your calendar will be provided, and others will be by your design. Often, just the experience of chopping up the school day and fitting in the periods for your subjects is enlightening. Chart your schedule, hang it near a clock, and stick to it.

Your schedule could also account for time spent before and after class. Fourth-grade teacher Heather Renz of Tom McCall Elementary School in Redmond, Oregon, ensures that her students make the most of every minute they spend in school with her "Mastery Club" (http://www2.redmond.k12.or.us/mccall/renz/masteryclub.htm). Before and after school and during recess, the students research the answers to eighty-four questions that pertain to all subject areas. They submit their results to receive a certificate and placement on her "wall of fame." The classroom activity is so popular that Renz has published her list of questions on-line, and teachers from far away have borrowed and tweaked her concept for their own classrooms.

Another matter to consider in your schedule is what will happen when you are not in class and a substitute teacher must handle it. Don't allow time with a substitute to be less meaningful than a regular school day. Provide detailed plans when possible. Have a folder with a seating chart, an explanation of classroom procedures, and appropriate lesson plans at the ready for emergencies. You may not always anticipate an absence, so ask a colleague who knows your classroom to be a backup for unforeseen circumstances, and offer to do the same for him or her. Your substitute folder should include the names of these backup teachers who can help, as well as students who are capable and reliable classroom assistants. Fill your substitute folder with meaningful activities that can be done at any time during the year—for example, the *Time For Kids* magazine with a lesson to practice determining importance within nonfiction text, or a math and science graphing activity involving classroom materials that are always on hand. Ira knows that a day left to word searches and videos must be avoided if at all possible. You should also have a written description of your procedures and routines. The more information with which you can arm substitute teachers, the more likely they will be able to "fake it until they can make it" with your students.

A Calendar

Next, be ready to look ahead. For this, you will need a calendar. Choose one with space to record ideas for reflection and improving yesterday's lesson, schoolwide events, test days, personal appointments, and anything else that you need to remember. Make a habit of checking your calendar each day, as often as is appropriate.

Also, consider providing your students (and at the same time their parents) with their own monthly calendars that contain instructional themes for the month, assignments, quizzes, tests, special events, etc. If students are old enough to manage their calendars independently, you can let them track this information for themselves. Consider having students staple the calendars to the inside covers of their notebooks for quick reference. Your calendar will visually map the teaching time that will be open to you and what you plan to do with it over the course of each month.

Routines and Rules

Anyone who has spent a day in a classroom knows that students are absolute creatures of habit. They take comfort in the expected, and they will bring to your attention—as well as to the poor substitute teacher who is present for only a day—any deviation from tradition. Clearly, having set routines for lunch count, storing materials, entering the classroom in the morning, coming and going as a class, distributing papers, collecting homework, etc. saves time. Teach and practice these routines with your students and capitalize on their willingness to help with classroom routines by appointing helpers. All children should be involved as much as possible in maintaining the smooth operation of the classroom.

Ira has learned that the time he spends teaching and practicing quality classroom procedures and expectations will pay off in increased instructional time down the road. He understands and also wants his students to understand that behavioral standards are just as important as academic standards. Ken Tankerous simply expects children to know how to behave in his class. When they make mistakes, he'll swiftly administer consequences. His method works for some students, but not for all of them, and it certainly inhibits relationships. Ken also wastes crucial instructional time delivering consequences to chronic offenders, and some students test Ken's limits simply to gain attention. Ken will eventually remove them from the classroom, but then the students' instruction will be lost. Ken tries to preserve his instructional schedule for the rest of the class, but both he and the children are often frustrated by all of the drama.

Kay will make a mistake on the other end of the continuum. While Ken's classroom rules are hidden and can be harsh, hers are just rumors. She'll bend her rules in the name of relationship-building on nearly a daily basis. She will allow the children to distract her from her instructional mission by telling stories and sharing personal details of their lives. What Ken lacks in relationships, Kay will more than make up for. But her nurturing nature causes her and her students to fall further and further behind. Ira observes these two extremes and strives for a balance between the health of the relationships in his classroom, student ownership of the classroom expectations, and the SMARTI goals he has created.

Your "Stop Doing" List

When Doug Reeves tells educators that they have to pull the weeds before planting the flowers, he is warning them about becoming bogged down with all sorts of classroom clutter. Assemblies, announcements, cutting, coloring, pasting, dittos, and other projects—without purpose—can take on a life of their own. He encourages teachers to participate in a fifteen-minute drill at a staff meeting to develop a "stop doing" list (Reeves 2005). On a large sheet of poster board, create a table as depicted in Exhibit 14.

In the left side of this table, staff members first list all of the initiatives adopted over the last five years. Second, in the right side of the table they list all those initiatives that have been evaluated and eliminated because they were not working or were not related to standards or to SMARTI goals. In

EXHIBIT 14

Initiative Fatigue: *Fifteen-minute drill*

Initiatives and activities we have started in the last five years:	Initiatives and activities we have deliberately reviewed and terminated:
(Use other side of page if necessary)	

most schools, staff members discover that they rarely *stop doing* anything. They simply throw new initiatives on the initiative cart that they are already pulling behind them. Try the same activity yourself, using your classroom initiatives. And, if you are a new teacher and don't need a "stop-doing" list, create a "don't even think about it" list!

Ira has developed the discipline to stop doing anything and everything that doesn't impact the real work, student achievement, his SMARTI goals, attendance, and graduation. Ken Tankerous does whatever he wants, just like he's always done. Ken will dismiss some standards because they do not reflect what he believes to be important knowledge. He already has his curriculum, and it's the resource he was given. It's called a textbook.

Kay Serra will likely try every new thing that she reads about on her teacher blog or in her instructor magazines. She is constantly on the lookout for a silver-bullet program or lesson. While the activities and ideas that she brings to her class are engaging and fun for the students, they may not be aligned to standards. Kay finds her activities and then "correlates" them to a standard, rather than working to understand her standards and then crafting her instruction.

There is a funny story making the rounds about a teacher who popped open a ceiling tile and cut the wires to her classroom loudspeaker. When asked why she never responded to intercom announcements, she would look puzzled and say that her loudspeaker seemed to be broken. She used the extra bits of uninterrupted learning time to focus her students on studying math word problems, and reading novels, and several other activities that captured her students' interest, and she raised their achievement levels significantly. Whether this is a true story, an urban legend, or wishful thinking, we may never know, but the tale is food for thought.

Our Overstuffed but Undernourished Curriculum

Goals, schedules, calendars, and routines are necessary, but are not sufficient for effective instruction. No matter how focused, organized, and efficient you become, and no matter how fast you talk, the notion that the school year offers you the time to finish a 400-page textbook, or all students ample time to become proficient in fifty, sixty, or, in some states, eighty standards per subject is simply not true.

There is a huge contradiction in our schools. We read books, attend workshops, and make endless references to "teaching for understanding" and "drilling down," but we continue to ask teachers to "cover" countless standards. The result: Teachers develop a "if it's Tuesday, this must be double-digit addition" pace and end up covering everything and teaching almost nothing. Coverage is probably the single greatest enemy of understanding (Gardner 2006).

Teachers attending our workshops constantly complain that they are too busy to teach. Here are just a few of the things they say: "I wish I had the time to do that, but I don't," or "My plate is too full right now," or "Implementing that new teaching strategy has me thinking—about a career change." And when we ask an audience of teachers if they are sure that they are teaching their state standards, they laugh and say that they are certain the state standards are in their textbooks, because, "Our textbooks have 400 pages. Heck! Everything is in there."

Their point is dramatically illustrated in the Third International Mathematics and Science Survey (TIMSS). When U.S. textbooks were compared to textbooks in other countries, dramatic differences were uncovered. U.S. fourth- and eighth-grade mathematics textbooks presented between thirty and thirty-five topics, whereas textbooks in Germany and Japan presented twenty and ten topics, respectively. U.S. fourth-, eighth-, and twelfth-grade science textbooks addressed between fifty and sixty-five topics; Japanese textbooks between five and fifteen topics; and German textbooks, seven topics. In other words, U.S. mathematics textbooks presented 175 percent as many topics as German textbooks and 350 percent as many topics as Japanese textbooks! And, instead of being troubled by our books that schools can't afford, teachers can't finish, and students can't carry, we put wheels on everyone's school bags. Our science textbooks contain more than nine times as many topics as German textbooks and more than four times as many topics as Japanese textbooks (Marzano 2003).

Do these bigger books translate into more teaching, higher test scores, and more learning on international tests? No, they don't! German and Japanese students dramatically and consistently outperform U.S. students on international mathematics and science tests (Schmidt, McKnight, Raizen 1996).

Probably the most dramatic evidence that teachers are too busy to teach comes from the educational consulting group Learning 24-7 (2005). They sent a team of teachers across the country to observe other teachers. They found some interesting information, shown in Exhibit 15.

These were not *bad* teachers being observed. They were just incredibly *busy* teachers being observed. Just like you, they went to the "No Worksheets Workshop." They held hands with the other participants and sang the "ditto is a five-letter word" song. They wanted to do better. They wanted to create one of the performance assessments Doug Reeves discussed, or the instructional unit that Robert Marzano demonstrated. However, hectic classrooms and an overwhelming number of standards sabotaged all of their good intentions. They did not have the time, the energy, or the permission to implement the new strategies they had learned. They were too busy to teach and too busy to think!

EXHIBIT 15
What's Going On in Our Classrooms?

Behavior	Percentage of Classrooms Where This Was Evident
Clear learning objective	4%
Teaching to mastery	0%
Higher order thinking	3%
Academic dialogue or discussion	0.5%
Students required to speak in complete sentences	0%
Worksheets	52%
Lecture	31%
Fewer than one-half of students engaged	82%
Evidence of student writing/editing/rubrics	0%

Given the limited time you have with your students, extraordinary teaching has become more and more an issue of deciding what you *won't* teach rather than what you *will* teach. You cannot do it all (Jacobs 1997). It takes time to write a good story, understand the difference between an observation and an inference, or learn double-digit addition. We complain that students don't remember what they learned, but the truth is they never really learned it in the brief time we covered it.

To be sure, some people will object to the idea of teaching less. They'll stamp their feet and send letters to the editor, and say we should finish the books, teach all of the standards, and eliminate things like art, music, and physical education. In these schools, recess becomes a rumor and kindergarten and preschoolers get drilled on academic skills usually reserved for first and second graders. The expression, "Let them eat cake," is updated to read, "Let them nap, sing, and play at home." But even these silly changes would not be enough. Schools would have to increase the amount of instructional time by about 71 percent to cover the current load of state standards (Marzano 2007).

If our priority is for students to think deeply and explore ideas thoughtfully, then the logical and unavoidable answer is: Teachers, principals, superintendents, and departments of education will have to make a choice between either coverage or learning. Next, we'll demonstrate how to prioritize your curriculum for learning. Exhibits 16 and 17 provide examples of this process by focusing on two types of events that are common in schools—fundraisers and assemblies. These examples show how Ira would handle such events. Exhibit 18 is for *you* to fill out as part of the following Journal Activity.

Journal Activity

- *What are the schoolwide events that go on in your school that are not focused on the standards? Is there a way to avoid some of these activities or incorporate a standard or two? Is there a culminating performance assessment for measurement hiding in your school's bicycle safety program?*

- *What's your Ira Quotient (IQ)? Examine how Ira handled the first two events (Exhibits 16 and 17). Then fill in the data for the third event (Exhibit 18).*

EXHIBIT 16

The Fundraiser

I know . . .

About my students:
- They are apathetic about assembly.
- They need to know the "hows" and "whats" about the fundraiser.

About my colleagues:
- Three colleagues don't go to the fundraiser, but present information to their students.

About my parents:
- It's a PTA-supported event.
- PTA is very active.
- My parents also need to know the details of the fundraiser.

I think . . .
- I'm worried that my directions about the fundraiser will be different than those given at the assembly.
- Parents don't like two out of the three teachers who don't go to the assembly.
- Will not going hurt my reputation with parents? What will not going cost me?

I do . . .
- Give the principal my plan for sharing information with students to assure his support.
- Send home reminders of the fundraiser in the weekly newsletter to demonstrate support to parents.
- Skip the assembly.

The Bullying Assembly

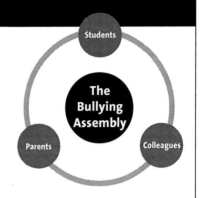

I know ...

About my students:
• Students survey showed that bullying is a high concern.

About my colleagues:
• Safety is a building goal.
• Everyone goes to this assembly.

About my parents:
• Safety is always a priority.
• PTA supports this program.

I think ...
• It's a shared goal for all.
• It has a high student interest.

I do ...
• Capitalize on the shared priority and tie into content academic (i.e., writing assignments).
• Attend the assembly.

EXHIBIT 18

Your Own School Event

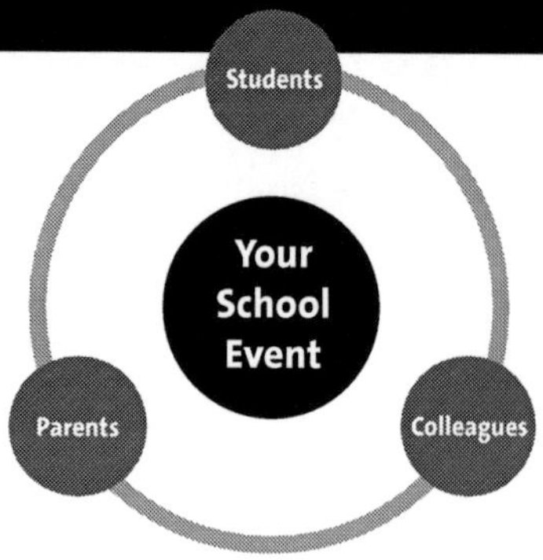

I know . . .

About my students:
-
-
-
-

About my colleagues:
-
-
-
-

About my parents:
-
-
-
-

I think . . .
-
-
-
-
-
-

I do . . .
-
-
-
-
-

Look at your school calendar and identify a future school event. Use the template in Exhibit 18 to determine how this event fits into *your* calendar.

Thinking about daily priorities and whether you attend assemblies is important to your personal sense of urgency for the year. However, there is a bigger idea that you must consider. *What is the sense of academic urgency with your students, parents, and colleagues? And, even bigger—how can you influence that culture?* Test your Ira Quotient (IQ) and try completing the Academic Urgency template (Exhibit 19) with data from your own situation; create your "to do's" for increasing the urgency for student success in your school.

EXHIBIT 19

Academic Urgency

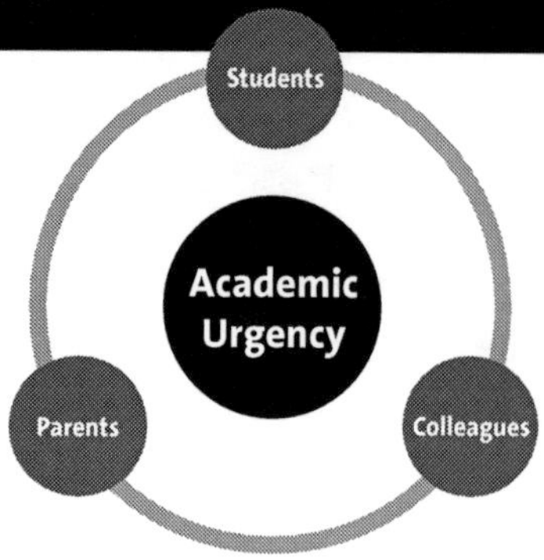

I know . . .

About my students:
- (Ira might list the tardiness issue in his room.)
-
-
-
-

About my colleagues:
- (Ira might list the number of loudspeaker interruptions.)
-
-
-
-

About my parents:
- (Ira might list the lack of parental cooperation with homework.)
-
-
-
-

I think . . .
-
-
-
-
-

I do . . .
-
-
-
-
-

Not All Standards Are Created Equal

Before we get into a discussion about prioritizing what you teach, we need to define some terms. Unfortunately, words like "benchmarks," "standards," "objectives," "indicators," and "expectancies" can represent vastly different things. In some states, "standards" describe general expectations of what students will learn during their kindergarten through grade twelve schooling, while in other states, "standards" describe very specific grade-level performance. This is confusing.

Whatever terms your state uses, the process starts with a very general description of what a student should learn from kindergarten through twelfth grade. In some states this is called the "standard." The terms "benchmark" or "grade span" are usually used to describe skills that students should acquire as they pass through an age or grade range, like kindergarten through grade two, or grade six through grade eight. The following benchmarks were developed by Ohio and Florida educators and represent what students from each of these states should know and be able to do by the end of their middle elementary grade programs:

- Model and use commutative and associative properties for addition and multiplication (Ohio, grades three through four).
- Select from a variety of simple strategies, including the use of phonics, word structure, context clues, self-questioning, confirming simple predictions, retelling, and using visual cues to identify words and construct meaning from various texts, illustrations, graphics, and charts (Florida, grades three through five).

Benchmarks and grade-span skills can contain multiple concepts. When these concepts are assigned to a specific grade, we have what are typically called indicators, objectives, or grade-level expectancies. These are concepts that students should know or skills that they should be able to demonstrate in a particular grade. The following indicators for Ohio fourth-grade and Florida third-grade students represent one of the concepts gleaned from their benchmarks:

- Use associative properties to simplify and perform left-to-right computations (5×47) (Ohio, fourth grade).
- Uses context clues (for example, known words, phrases, structures) to infer the meaning of new and unfamiliar words, including synonyms, antonyms, and homophones (Florida, third grade).

As a teacher, it is important to understand how your grade indicators support the grade-span outcomes and ultimately a K-12 standard, but most of your work will be at the indicator level. *Indicators are the instructional concepts that should form your individual lessons.* And most state tests measure proficiency at this level.

Exhibit 20 visually depicts the relationships between the commonly used terms of "standards," "benchmarks/grade spans," and "indicators."

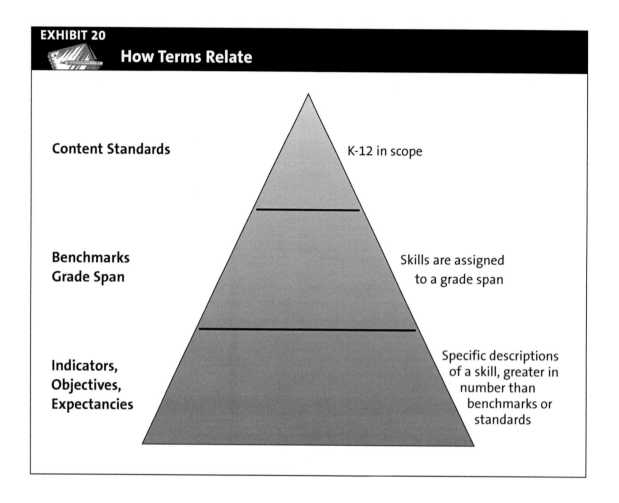

EXHIBIT 20

How Terms Relate

Content Standards — K-12 in scope

Benchmarks Grade Span — Skills are assigned to a grade span

Indicators, Objectives, Expectancies — Specific descriptions of a skill, greater in number than benchmarks or standards

Two Types of Indicators

Another important distinction needs to be made before we can prioritize what we teach. Virtually all state indicators have a pattern. There are two types.

The first type of indicator we refer to as "one and done." "One and done" indicators are those that can be taught and assessed in a neat little package. It may take one lesson or it may take four. Our point is, you will teach this indicator to mastery and move on. "One and done" indicators are usually content indicators. Here are some examples of "one and done" indicators:

- Identify and describe reflections and rotations in geometry.
- Explain why elections are used to select leaders and decide issues.
- Describe the relationship between rocks, minerals, and soil.
- Describe the type of government expressed in the Declaration of Independence.

- Read, write, and identify common percents including 10 percent, 20 percent, 25 percent, 30 percent , 40 percent, 50 percent, 60 percent, 70 percent, 75 percent, 80 percent, 90 percent, and 100 percent.
- Recognize the difference between the meanings of connotation and denotation.
- Identify the meanings of abbreviations.

The second type of indicator cannot, and should not, be taught just once. We call these "long and lingering" indicators. Grant Wiggins and Jay McTighe (1998) refer to them as "big ideas," while Larry Ainsworth (2003a) calls them "power standards." These indicators often involve process, rather than content, skills. They can also represent the application or synthesis of a "one and done" indicator. "Long and lingering" indicators represent skills that last from one academic year to the next. They can be applied across the curriculum, and if students are proficient on these indicators, the teacher who has your students next year will forever be grateful to you.

Here are a few examples of "long and lingering" indicators:

- Identify main ideas and find information to support particular ideas.
- Understand how scientific theories are used to explain and predict natural phenomena.
- Interpret and create charts and graphs.

When teachers are asked what is essential for success in their classes, they rarely respond with a list of "one and done" indicators. A teacher will usually respond that students should have skills in applying reading comprehension strategies. Students should be able to make predictions, compare and contrast, summarize, and make inferences. This wish list is usually short, sweet, and surprisingly similar, whether you ask an elementary language arts teacher, or a high school science teacher. "Long and lingering" indicators are skills that are necessary for success at the next level of instruction, endure over time, and have leverage across subject areas. These are the skills upon which your instruction should focus. These are the skills that you will teach and assess continually.

Exhibit 21 represents both types of indicators.

We are not suggesting that you ignore "one-and-done" indicators; we are simply suggesting that you *prioritize*. Shift the bulk of your teaching and collaboration to the indicators that deserve and require more time. The limited instructional time you have with your students means that you must separate the critical indicators from indicators that are less important. Different teachers will make different choices, depending on the needs of their students, about how they will teach the "one and done" indicators. But every teacher should ensure that every student learns the "long and lingering" indicators.

Let's be honest: You'll never teach the entire textbook or the entire curriculum. You already prioritize your indicators. Currently, your decision about what to teach is based on sequence—you teach

EXHIBIT 21

Two Types of Indicators

"One and Done" Indicators	"Long and Lingering" Indicators
Skip-count by 2, 5, and 10 to develop multiplicative reasoning and notational. *(New Mexico, Math, Grade 2)*	Display data in a variety of formats. *(New Mexico, Math, Grade 2)*
Know that energy can be described as stored energy (potential) or energy of motion (kinetic). *(Florida, Science, Grade 5)*	Understand how changes in the environment affect organisms. *(Florida, Science, Grade 5)*
Explain how colonization, westward expansion, immigration, and advances in transportation and communication changed geographic patterns in the United States. (Ohio, Social Studies, Grade 8)	Select events and construct a multiple-tier time line to show relationships among events. *(Ohio, Social Studies, Grade 8)*
Prepare a bibliography of reference materials for a report using a variety of consumer, workplace, and public documents. *(California, Language Arts, Grade 10)*	Extend ideas presented in primary or secondary sources through original analysis, evaluation, and elaboration. *(California, Language Arts, Grade 10)*

the indicators that are listed early in your curriculum document, or that occur in the first half of the textbook. You do not teach—you "cover" or "mention"—the indicators that occur late in those documents. Why? Because you run out of time. So our question is, what's better: prioritizing by design or prioritizing by default?

There is no need for a fancy chart to prioritize your indicators. Simply open up your standards book, read the indicators aloud to discuss them, and write an "O" or an "L" in the margin. Exhibit 22 shows a sample classification using Ohio's standards. Doing this activity as a grade-level team would be great. Remember the following when classifying your indicators: A "long and lingering" indicator will probably never have the word "gerund" in it. Knowing when or where the Declaration of Independence was signed: "one and done." Knowing *why* the Declaration of Independence was signed: "long and lingering."

EXHIBIT 22

Sample Classification Using Ohio's Standards

ACADEMIC CONTENT STANDARDS

		Indicator Type
Geometry and Spatial Sense Standard		
Characteristics and Properties	1. Identify, describe, and model intersecting parallel and perpendicular lines and line segments; e.g., use straws or other material to model lines.	O
	2. Describe, classify, compare, and model two- and three-dimensional objects, using their attributes.	O
	3. Identify similarities and differences of quadrilaterals; e.g., squares, rectangles, parallelograms, and trapezoids.	O
	4. Identify and define triangles based on angle measures (equiangular, right, acute, and obtuse triangles) and side lengths (isosceles, equilateral, and scalene triangles).	O
Spatial Relationships	5. Describe points, lines, and planes; and identify models in the environment.	O
	6. Specify locations and plot ordered pairs on a coordinate plane, using first quadrant points.	O
Transformations and Symmetry	7. Identify, describe, and use reflections (flips), rotations (turns), and translations (slides) in solving geometric problems; e.g., use transformations to determine if two shapes are congruent.	O
Visualizations and Geometric Models	8. Use geometric models to solve problems in other areas of mathematics, such as number (multiplication/division) and measurement (area, perimeter, border).	L
Patterns, Functions, and Algebra Standard		
Use Patterns, Relations, and Functions	1. Use models and words to describe, extend, and make generalizations of patterns and relationships occurring in computation, numerical patterns, geometry, graphs, and other applications.	O
	2. Represent and analyze patterns and functions using words, tables, and graphs.	L
Use Algebraic Representation	3. Construct a table of values to solve problems associated with a mathematical relationship.	O
	4. Use rules and variables to describe patterns and other relationships.	L

Grade Four

O = "One & Done"   L = "Long & Lingering"

Let us close this section by acknowledging that there are other ways to prioritize indicators—to identify those that will receive powerful, thorough, and ongoing instruction. And last time we checked, prioritizing state indicators based on test results was not a crime. Before school begins, use your student test data to uncover indicators on which your students performed the poorest. Add those to your priority list. We're willing to bet that these indicators will usually be the same ones you listed as your "long and lingering" indicators.

However you prioritize, just do it. Here's the big question: If you only have enough time to teach twenty, maybe thirty, concepts per subject, shouldn't you use common sense, colleague input, and student data to make sure that you're teaching the biggest, baddest indicators on the block?

 SCOOP

For an excellent discussion of prioritizing indicators, please read Larry Ainsworth's books entitled *Power Standards* and *Unwrapping the Standards*.

Journal Activities

- Open up your standards book, read each indicator, and write an O ("one and done") and an L ("long and lingering") in the margin. Compare your work with a grade-level colleague.

- Review your students' test data to determine your class's weakest indicators. How did these indicators match up with your "long and lingering" indicators?

- Use your template (Exhibit 23) to think about and develop a plan to increase your students', colleagues', and parents' understanding of state standards.

EXHIBIT 23

Standards

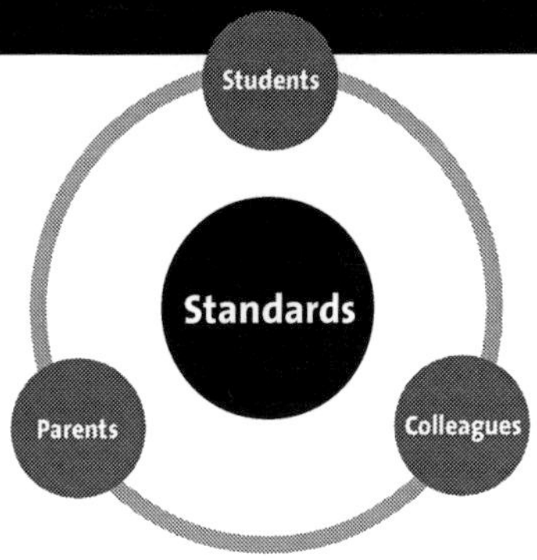

I know . . .

About my students:
- (Ira might list the students' disconnect across content areas.)
-
-
-
-

About my colleagues:
- (Ira might list that the board adopted materials that are monitored by the principal.)
-
-
-
-

About my parents:
- (Ira might list that his parents expect students to bring books home every night.)
-
-
-
-

I think . . .
-
-
-
-

I do . . .
-
-
-
-

Engagement

Now that you have decided *what to teach*, it's time to think about *how to teach*.

The good news: Nearly thirty-five years of research provide the ingredients of effective teaching. Some great resources to have on your bookshelf include:

- *Making Standards Work* by Douglas Reeves
- *The Art and Science of Teaching* by Robert Marzano
- *The First Days of School* by Harry Wong and Rosemary Wong
- *Results Now* by Mike Schmoker
- *The Schools Our Children Deserve* by Alfie Kohn

One of the most surprising messages from the research on teaching is that high achievement should not necessarily be the target for which teachers aim. High achievement is usually a by-product. The million-dollar question: A by-product of what? And the answer is: Engagement! Remember all of the student interest data you collected? Here's where you'll use it!

Emotional Engagement

In *The Schools Our Children Deserve*, Alfie Kohn warns us, "The most immediate and pressing issue for students and teachers is not low achievement, but student disengagement" (page 128). The same rules that apply to the school playground apply to the classroom: Children do not work or play well with others whom they don't like, and they don't keep playing a game in which they always lose. In other words, your students will be engaged as long as the material is relevant, as long as they think someone cares and is there to help, and as long as they believe that there is a chance for them to be successful.

Think back to your days as an elementary or middle school student. Who were your best teachers? They may have shaved their heads, kissed a pig for fundraisers, or slept on the roof of the school building if every student read twenty books. But, more importantly, they proved that they were willing to go the distance to engage you and make you feel that they had a personal stake in your success. Even when you weren't excited about an assignment or a chapter in the book, that wasn't as important as the attitude you had toward the teacher and the class.

Here are some suggestions for fostering emotional engagement with your students:

- Meet students at the door in the morning.
- Take pictures of the students working, and display them.
- Smile, listen, and always stay calm.

- Use humor.
- Use words from students' lives—"sketchy," "tight," and "fly." (Note that words change quickly. The ones that are "in" this week will be "out" next week.) Also, use words that you have heard their parents or grandparents use ("persnickety," "turkey," and "bonkers").

Students look to us to build and model proper vocabulary. Add their words to your vocabulary, but also encourage them to add your words to their vocabulary.

- Volunteer to serve as a sponsor, advisor, or chaperone for after-school clubs, organizations, and events.
- Compliment students on what they are wearing.
- Make a point of watching at least one television program that your students watch.
- Be aware of video games they are playing, and their music and Internet culture.

Emotional engagement does not mean that you are a pushover. You still "own the room," and consistently and calmly enforce the rules, and look for opportunities to provide positive reinforcement. Think about some of the teachers you liked best as a student. We bet they weren't pushovers!

Academic Engagement

We have seen lots of things in our years of teaching, consulting, and traveling, including a polar bear riding a bicycle, but we have never seen a child who is "hooked on phonics." And, like your students, we think that the answer to the question "What fraction is larger—4/11 or 5/13?" is "Who cares?"

It only makes sense that the more engaging an assignment is, the more likely students are to immerse themselves in it and stick with it through completion. But what makes a task more interesting? What causes a student to be more engaged by one unit than another? How can you design work that will keep students' attention at the same time it draws them more deeply into the process of learning?

Engaging Scenarios

Teachers who are most successful in engaging students develop activities with students' interests in mind (Marzano 2007). Try to create units and assignments that relate to student's lives, are fun, and arouse their curiosity. The information gleaned from parents, surveys, and your morning meetings should provide you a treasure trove of material with which to work.

Doug Reeves (2004b) suggests using engaging scenarios to introduce your units. Rather than starting with, "Today we are going to learn how to determine the area of a rectangle," hold up a contract signed by the iconic pop star of the week. Pretend, with the class, that she is coming to give a concert, and her contract demands that the stage be 100 square feet, with security rope around three sides. Your class spends the rest of the morning working in small groups designing stages and computing how much rope they will need.

SCOOP

Remember that, while you're wondering how your students are doing in their work, they're wondering why they're doing it!

How about instruction that can be applied in real life? Most students are eager to do "grown-up things." Why not use their desire to act "grown up" to teach? What do grown-ups read? When do grown-ups use math? Older students might be hooked into reading or doing math by reading and discussing *USA Today* or helping you balance a checkbook. Showing students how a classroom activity is related to the world of work or money are sure bets to get their attention. Exhibit 24 shows some engaging scenarios that you might use to introduce your instruction.

Consider your students' interests and add some engaging scenarios of your own to Exhibit 24.

EXHIBIT 24

Engaging Scenarios

Elementary	Middle School	High School
You've been asked to design a new Nintendo game . . .	Your community is considering a teen curfew. Write a letter to the editor of the local newspaper . . .	Develop a concept map that will help your classmates . . .
You are on the committee to help our principal revise spirit week with new themes . . .	Develop a song lyric that describes your . . .	As a member of the Senate, make the case for or against allowing kids to vote at seventeen . . .
As crime scene investigators, let's sift through evidence to find out who borrowed our . . .	Some of the surrounding schools are switching to a school uniform policy . . .	You are trying to help your older brother decide if it's better to rent or buy a house . . .
Develop a movie script that is about searching for . . .	Design a game that teaches young students . . .	Write a report that describes working with . . .
A famous author wants you to write a different ending to his or her book . . .	Make a time line that shows the history of . . .	Draw a picture that will get students interested in . . .

Menus, Not Mandates

Another way to academically engage students is to provide them with choices—a menu of tasks rather than a single task. Menus allow students a degree of control over learning and allow you to offer challenging but achievable tasks to all of your students, regardless of their proficiency level (Reeves 2004b).

Let's imagine that you wanted to teach the following standard: *Describe and give examples of ways in which people interact with their physical environment, including use of land, location of communities, and design of shelters.*

Rather than requiring everyone to create a Venn diagram to compare and contrast a "big city" and a "wilderness region," you might offer students these choices:

Task 1— Draw a region map of a wilderness area or a big city.

Task 2— Write a letter to a friend back home in the city, describing your new life in the wilderness or your new life in a big city.

Task 3— Pretend that you are a real estate agent and design a wilderness brochure that encourages people to move from the city.

Task 4— Develop a skit entitled "A Typical Day Where I Live."

A menu of tasks is a great tool for individualizing student learning, meeting special needs and learning styles, and keeping all students engaged and interested. While the above example varied the tasks based on learning styles, you could also provide a menu of tasks based on difficulty level (skill building, test level, and advanced).

Guides on the Side

Supreme Court Justice Lewis Powell once defined pornography as, "I cannot say what it is, but I know it when I see it." Unfortunately, a similar definition of "good work" exists in far too many classrooms where the teacher says, "Good work: I cannot say what it is, but I know it when I see it." This definition leaves good student work a mystery—something that students guess at. The definition of good work is resolved only by the judgment of the teacher after the student has turned it in (Reeves 2004a).

Guides on the side take the opposite approach. They provide students and parents with a student-friendly definition, maybe even an example, of good work, before students begin the assignment (Reeves 2004b). So, in addition to asking students to write a letter describing their first day in the wilderness, or a big city, you could provide them with the following description of what a good letter should contain. You might even provide an example of a good letter. Examples of both are shown in Exhibit 25.

EXHIBIT 25

Examples of Guide on the Side and Proficient Work

Friendly Letter Guide on the Side

Assignment: Write a letter to a friend back home telling him or her about your first day in the wilderness of Wisconsin.

GUIDE ON THE SIDE:

- Letter is time-sequenced and includes morning, lunch, and evening activities.
- Use descriptive language. Be sure to use all five senses as you describe the day, to help the reader imagine it.
- Letter is between 75 and 100 words.
- Letter has no spelling errors.

Sample of Proficient Work:

Dear T.J.,

Well, we made it. The wagon didn't break down and we got to our new home in Wisconsin. There are lots of trees and lakes. The wind blowing through the trees sounds just like the ocean back home.

My first day here I had to get up real early, while it was still dark, to take care of the animals. Guess what? Pigs are not slimy, but you were right. They do smell funny!

I went fishing after lunch and watched my granddad hunt squirrels. It got cold at night, so we played games and read close to the fire. I did not see a bear.

Your friend,
Katherine

You might not include all of the components, scenarios, menus, scoring guides, and sample work all of the time, but you can always try to include some of them. And your students can help you create all of these tools.

See the performance assessment sample in Appendix D, and read Making Standards Work (Reeves 2004b) for step-by-step guidance on how to design and implement performance assessments.

Be a Hero, Dump the Zero

Another cause of student disengagement might be something much more basic than teaching techniques. It might be the way in which we assign grades (Reeves 2008a). Over the last twenty-some years, we have heard far too many students defend their disengagement by saying, "I'm not going to pass this class anyway, so why should I try?" or "This class is stupid."

While this attitude is undoubtedly disheartening to teachers and parents, from a psychologist's perspective, it is perfectly understandable. It's actually an effective defense mechanism. Students who don't think that they can do something discount the thing that they don't think they can do; i.e., "I think I can't do math or dance, so I decide that doing math or dancing is stupid." The alternative, admitting that the skill, class, or assignment is important and that I can't do it, would mean, "I am stupid."

Too many students are afraid of failing and looking dumb! Share your personal challenges with students. Make sure that students know that you struggle with new learning, too, and that the struggle is part of the reward. Tell them about the "D" you got in statistics! Tell them about your struggle to learn sign language, or how to play the piano. Model the behavior you wish them to exhibit .

Now, let's look at how grades can play a part in all of this. It's mid-September in Ken Tankerous's class and Elizabeth misses the deadline on a book report, earning an "F." If this "F" equals a zero, this "F" is a deadly grade. Unlike its cousin, the "D," this "F" is mathematically six times worse. While an A is worth ninety points, and a B, C, and D are worth eighty, seventy, and sixty points respectively, the F is worth zero. So, Elizabeth's mid-September lapse means that subsequent efforts to redeem herself are destined to fall short. If her grades for the rest of the quarter are eighty, seventy-five, and eighty-two, her average of fifty-nine is still an F (80 + 75 + 82 + 0 ÷ 4 = 59). Elizabeth, well aware of the law of averages, decides to spend her time passing notes rather than trying to pass the class. Ask her why, and she'll tell you that the class is "stupid!" Ken will tell you that she is an irresponsible student who needed to learn a lesson. It is, after all, what she earned.

In some schools, the chance of earning a zero has been eliminated. And, therefore the chance of being successful is increased. Teachers in these schools understand how heavily a zero can weigh on a student's final grade. The lowest score students can receive is as high as fifty or sixty-eight—even if they don't turn in assignments. Of course, this practice challenges the long-held philosophy that if you don't do the work, you shouldn't get the grade. Ira might reflect on what the assignment was intended to measure anyway.

Douglas Reeves, in a *Phi Delta Kappan* article, wrote, "A zero for work that is not turned in is punished much more severely than work that is done wretchedly and is worth a D" (Reeves 2004c). Some teachers avoid the zero by using only letter grades instead of numbers or points. Teachers and administrators need to begin dialogue and take a serious look at what the zero does to students. One grade should not cause a student to fail the entire course or dramatically change the final grade he or she receives.

Other schools have a different method of eliminating the effect of zeros. A review of the records of students who received failing grades led Principal David Chambers of Cantwell Sacred Heart of Mary High School to establish a mandatory homework study hall. When students at the Montebello, California, school did not submit homework assignments on time, they were required to make up the work during a study hall before or after school. Impressively, the GPA increased immediately by almost half of a grade point, and even the performance of the honor students improved. "We didn't consider the fact that honor students don't always do *their* homework," Chambers said. "Our honor roll went from 32 percent of our student body to over 50 percent." (Bafile March 2004).

About four weeks into the school year, Dotti Etzler, a business teacher at Francis Scott Key High School in Union Bridge, Maryland, discovered that eighteen students in one of her high-school-level business classes had already accumulated forty-one zeros on assignments. They weren't doing well for a simple reason—they weren't completing the work. So Etzler adopted an original approach to resolving the problem, a "no zeros" policy. Her students formed groups and encouraged each other to complete their missed work and continue to get all of their work turned in on time. She held homework "checks" and rewarded groups with no missed assignments delicious zero-shaped treats, like doughnuts and pizza. Students in the class improved their grades simply by submitting their work, and they displayed deeper understanding of the material and a better outlook on the course (Bafile August 2004).

In Ira's class, a student who completes the assignment, but performs below proficient earns a score of sixty-nine. A student who does not turn in the assignment earns a score of sixty-eight. This system allows him to distinguish between a student who does not understand the work and one who does not do the work. These are very different problems with very different answers. And in Ira's class, the consequences for *not* doing the work is *doing* the work!

Journal Activities

• Look at your lesson plan for next week and develop an engaging scenario for one assignment, based upon what you know about your students.

• Test your Ira Quotient (IQ). What does your data tell you about what your students, parents, and colleagues think about grading? Does your grading philosophy match your players? Use Exhibit 26 to fill in your answers.

EXHIBIT 26

Grading Practices

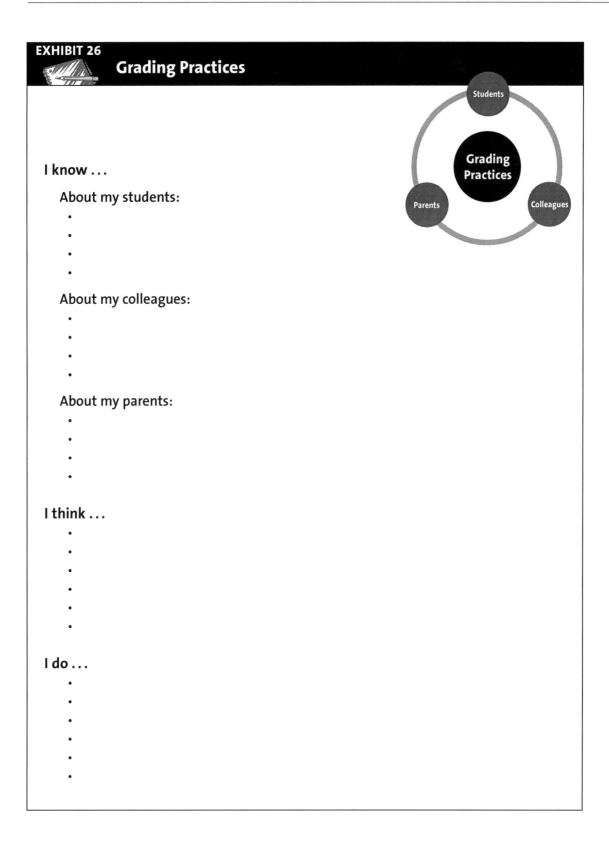

I know ...

    About my students:

-
-
-
-

    About my colleagues:

-
-
-
-

    About my parents:

-
-
-
-

I think ...

-
-
-
-
-
-

I do ...

-
-
-
-
-
-

Teaching as a Team Sport

When historians get around to listing the most astonishing discoveries about student achievement, there are two findings that won't make their list:

1. An effective teacher has more impact on student achievement than all other factors combined.

2. When teachers get together to talk in concrete, precise language about instruction and student work, their teaching dramatically improves and student achievement rises (Schmoker 2006).

Sadly, what might make our historians' list of astonishing discoveries is that we knew it was all about teaching and collaboration, yet we rarely collaborated in our schools.

The irony isn't troubling; it's frightening! We value teaching our students to work together and to learn from one another, but we don't model this behavior for them. We sing the praises of *two heads being better than one*, while we ignore the expertise of our colleagues and field experts. We expect teachers to hone their skills while incarcerated in a cafeteria for eight hours of mandatory, districtwide professional development. Aside from such events, it is the norm for teachers to work in isolation like independent contractors, sharing only the refrigerator and the parking lot. Each classroom is its own "microcosm."

We recently surveyed 427 teachers in grades kindergarten through twelve. The teachers were from public schools in Florida, Michigan, and Ohio (Crouse and White 2008). Here's what they told us about collaboration in their schools (see Exhibit 27):

Even though 85 percent of the teachers thought collaboration improved instruction (Question 1), our remaining questions uncovered an alarming disconnect between "knowing and doing." While teachers clearly understood that collaboration was important, 44 percent felt like they were "on their own" when it came to improving student achievement (Question 2). Nineteen percent of the surveyed teachers did not think that their materials or instruction matched their same-grade colleagues, while another 12 percent were not sure (Question 3). And, nearly half of the teachers did not see their school's calendars, curriculum maps, or scope and sequence charts helping their situation (Question 4). Perhaps it should not come as a surprise that almost half of our surveyed teachers would not like to see their own children become teachers. Why not? Maybe because for them it is a lonely profession (Question 5).

EXHIBIT 27

Teachers' Survey

In my opinion ...	Strongly Disagree	Disagree	Agree	Strongly Agree	Don't Know
1. Instruction improves dramatically when teachers routinely get together to discuss assessment results and teaching strategies.	1%	10%	50%	35%	4%
2. I feel like I'm on my own when it comes to improving the achievement of my class.	7%	46%	33%	11%	3%
3. My instructional materials and practices match those of my grade-level colleagues.	1%	18%	57%	12%	12%
4. Our current curriculum guide, calendar, or scope and sequence ensures that teachers are teaching the same thing at the same time.	4%	40%	43%	4%	9%
5. I would be thrilled if my son/daughter decided to become a teacher.	9%	34%	31%	11%	15%

Data Teams and Professional Learning Communities Are ...

Richard Dufour brought "professional learning communities" (PLCs) to prominence while he was a principal twenty-five years ago at Adlai Stevenson High School in Illinois. Small groups of teachers would meet weekly to create common formative assessments, analyze results, discuss strategies for improvement, and brainstorm creative units and lesson plans. Rather than a mishmash of chores, complaints, and group therapy, these meetings focused on three questions: what's working with our students, what isn't working with them, and which students need extra help (Dufour and Eaker 1998).

Was all this transparency and collaboration effective? Adlai Stevenson High School's name has appeared on the U.S. Department of Education's Blue Ribbon list four times—an honor shared by only two other schools nationwide. Every year, more than 3,000 educators visit the school to see PLCs in action. And today, professional learning communities, or, as they are also called, Data Teams, are thought to be the most promising strategy for improving instruction and student performance (Reeves 2004b; Schmoker 2006).

What makes these teams so powerful and empowering? It's this simple fact: you do not become an extraordinary teacher alone. But—don't get nervous—the journey is less about attaining perfection, and probably more about being a better teacher today than you were yesterday, about acknowledging imperfection and looking for competency and complementaries among your colleagues. Data Teams allow you to magnify your strengths, and work with other teachers who provide different but equally important strengths. Therefore, the math teacher who is a ninja at number sense may not be an expert on geometry. But the teacher across the hall cannot wait to share her engaging activity for scalene and isosceles triangles. While no single person will possess every dimension of an extraordinary teacher, the team is more likely to have all of them. And when teachers come together and talk about teaching, they realize that improvement is something they can generate, rather than something that is Power-Pointed out to them by so-called experts.

Data Teams Are Not . . .

Sometimes schools think that they have Data Teams, but they don't. They'll get together and talk about assemblies, field trips, lunch duty, and various "housekeeping" issues. These topics are important, but remember—real teacher work has to focus on what's being taught, its relationship to standards, how students are learning and behaving, and what needs to be done to get all students to improve. Effective Data Teams are groups of teachers who believe that they are collectively responsible for student success.

We recently spent two days working with a group of teachers on data analysis. That evening, logging on to our computer, we saw the following message:

Hello,

My name is Lisa. I was in your class on Thursday, and I understood you to say that you often helped schools develop plans to help them improve student achievement and student behavior. I would like your opinion on Data Teams. Our school is not showing growth and our Data Team has gone from being a book club to an opportunity to share meatloaf recipes.

Sincerely,
Lisa C.

While reading and discussing a book might be a good starting point for some teams, it should never be viewed as the culminating event! What, if instead of just reading a book, teachers collectively determined how to apply what they read to benefit students? We cannot imagine anything more frustrating than reading about bold changes in the way we might work and then not doing something about the way we work.

Data Teams are not recipe or book clubs, and they're not code for forms, flow charts, and spreadsheets. Sometimes developing and filling in these tools will occupy teachers for meeting, after meeting, after meeting. Taken to extremes, these activities can be a massive exercise in missing the point.

Forms are simply a way to structure the conversation so that all members participate, stay focused, and comply with group norms. Agendas that set time limits and topic boundaries can be especially helpful with hard-to-discuss topics by providing structure and psychological safety. They also can come in handy if one or two members monopolize the discussion or elbow others out of the discussion. Forms and agendas may help teachers spell out ground rules and expectations for their work, including how consensus is defined, how conflicts will be resolved, and how time will be spent. But they are not the real work, and if forms get in the way, change them or get rid of them!

How to Implement Data Team Techniques

Developing a Data Team, or at least a Data Team attitude, takes work and intentionality. It's unrealistic to think that you can flip your school to Data Team thinking overnight. Instead, take small steps that can start paving the way for active collaboration between teachers. The goal is to "get every brain in the game".

- Approach teachers like Ira, whose skills you respect, and ask them to observe your teaching and offer some suggestions on your methods. This takes courage!

- Ask to sit in on the class of an "Ira." Say something as simple as, "I always hear students leaving your class still discussing what you taught. I'd love to see how you get that level of engagement. Do you mind if I sit in on one of your classes to observe?" Or, "I noticed your students mastered this week's indicator. What are you doing?"

- Ask colleagues about conferences or workshops that they've attended. Mention an article you've read that they may find interesting. Share a brochure on a workshop in another teacher's area of expertise.

- Don't think that because you are the "rookie" you have nothing to contribute. The flow of information doesn't always go from experienced teacher to new teacher. Just as you value the child in your class who asks pertinent questions, your questions are essential to the growth of yourself and your colleagues. Your questions encourage more experienced teachers to consider practices and the basis for them. You are also likely to hold the most current knowledge of cutting-edge educational research that can and should be discussed.

- If you and your colleagues are initially reluctant to talk about student achievement, common assessments, and lessons, you may find it safer to discuss and collaborate on student behavioral issues, like reducing the number of office referrals or the number of bus incidents. So start there!

EXHIBIT 28

Suggestions for Data Team Activities

What you might do:	Why you would do these things:
Collaboratively score student work	Develop common understandings of the indicator
Analyze student data on a standard	
Identify lessons for remediation or enrichment	Pre-testing to plan instruction
Adjust lessons	Establish a common rigor
Share lessons	Select exemplars to share
Inform consistent grading procedures	

• If you are considering starting or reviving a Data Team in your school, remember—simple plans work best. Exhibit 28 provides modest suggestions for activities in which your Data Team could engage.

Journal Activity

• *Now test your Ira Quotient (IQ) by thinking about Data Teams in your situation and how you might influence their creation or success. Use Exhibit 29 as your template.*

EXHIBIT 29

Data Teams

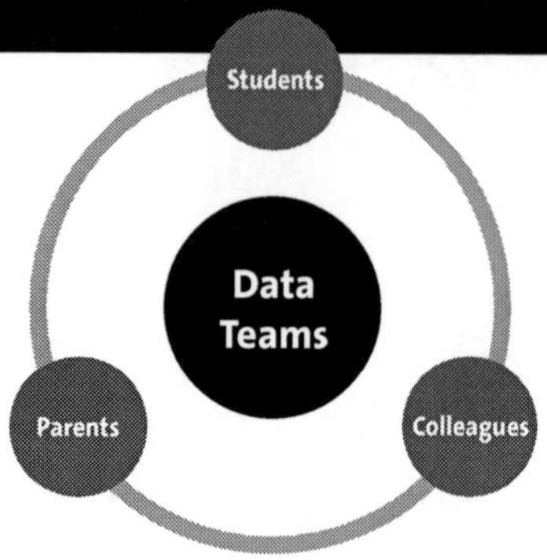

I know . . .

About my students:
- (Ira might list the fact that his students do poorly when a sub is there, so being out of class is a problem.)
-
-
-
-

About my colleagues:
- (Ira might list that book studies are popular, but money is tight.)
-
-
-
-

About my parents:
- (Ira might list that they believe teachers belong in the classroom.)
-
-
-
-

I think . . .
-
-
-
-
-

I do . . .
-
-
-
-
-

Becoming Extraordinary

Well, we're at the end of this book. We hope that you have learned these long and lingering ideas:

- Extraordinary teachers are reflective teachers.
- Open up, share, and learn from your students, their parents, and your colleagues.
- Expect great things from yourself, your students, and the other players.
- Prioritize. At the risk of sounding morbid, your days are numbered.

Avoid the frustration trap! Improvement is slow—at first. Here are some facts of life about improvement:

- Teachers and schools that moved from poor to better or good to extraordinary had no silver-bullet program and didn't change overnight.
- Principals, consultants, or books did not "motivate" teachers—their teachers were self-motivated.
- There's no connection between rants and raves and improvement. Believing that fear drives change isn't only preposterous, it's poisonous!
- Technology, forms, and flowcharts can be important, but they come into play only after improvement has already started.
- Extraodinary teachers and schools aren't the result of a dramatic event. There was no miracle moment (cue the trumpets) when a room full of teachers leapt from their workshop seats and shouted they'd been "Bob Marzanoed."

Instead, an attitude that was reflective, down to earth, and committed to high achievement, high support, and high expectations kept everyone on track for the long haul. Extraordinary is always the triumph of the tortoise over the hare, the victory of stick-to-itiveness over the quick-fix and flavor-of-the-month initiative. Change is fast and easy; improvement is slower and harder!

Hopefully, we have shown that being extraordinary doesn't mean that you have to butt heads with your principal every morning before the bell rings. Engagement, high expectations, collaboration, and even prioritizing what you teach, shouldn't require a coup. Nor does extraordinary mean that you have to be serious all the time. Smiling and laughing don't mean that you aren't thinking and teaching.

We began this book telling you that we did not have answers. Instead, we offered some modest suggestions for you to consider as you think about your teaching, your students, their parents, and your colleagues. Just as Ira does, you recognize that answers are something you have to generate based on your data, rather than something that's handed to you in a speech or a book. The person with the problem is usually the person with the answer! As your data change, so will your answers.

Once you realize that, you'll probably modify our reflective template in Appendix C, because your data require a different model. You'll also probably never laminate anything for the rest of your life. Two sure signs that you are on your way to being extraordinary!

Communication Log

Phone Call Record					
Date	Time	Placed By	Name of Parent	Child's Name and Reason for Call	Notes

APPENDIX B
Introduction to DIBELS

The Dynamic Indicators of Basic Early Literacy Skills (DIBELS) are a set of standardized, individually administered measures of literacy development in grades K-6. They are designed to be short fluency assessments used to regularly monitor the development of pre-reading and reading skills. DIBELS data are predictive of future reading success and are used to identify students in need of early intervention.

DIBELS scores place students into risk categories that produce instructional recommendations for teachers who direct the intensity of intervention.

DIBELS Web Site

The DIBELS Web site is located at http://dibels.uoregon.edu/.
It includes descriptions and tutorials on each of the measures, technical reports, logistical information on implementing DIBELS in a school, and contact information for trainers. The measures themselves are available for download and use, free from the Web site (http://dibels.uoregon.edu/measures/materials.php).

APPENDIX C
Reflective Teaching Template

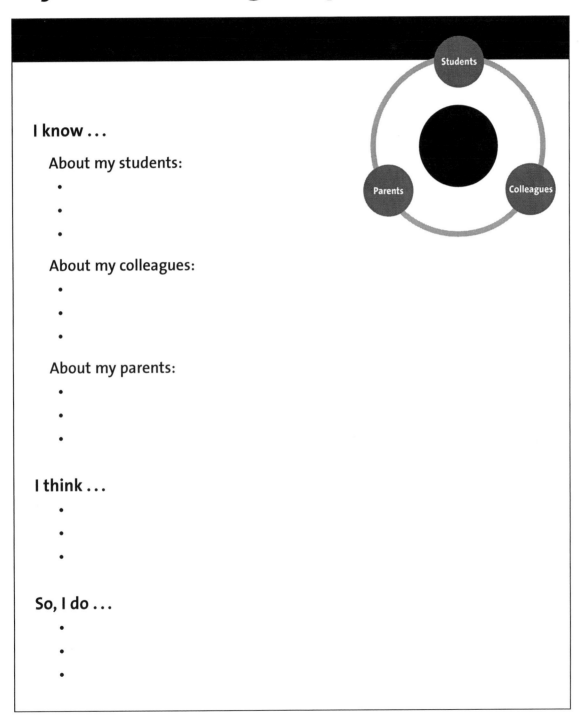

I know . . .

About my students:

-
-
-

About my colleagues:

-
-
-

About my parents:

-
-
-

I think . . .

-
-
-

So, I do . . .

-
-
-

APPENDIX D

Performance Assessment Sample

Secret Agents

Benchmark Grades: Upper Elementary

Summary:
Students practice basic arithmetic and some pre-algebra operations by coding and decoding several messages.

Key Words:
Arithmetic operations
Code
Decode
Pre-algebra

ASSESS

Information for the Teacher

Task Description

This assessment involves several levels of elementary math ability and introduces some pre-algebra concepts. Tasks 1 and 2 reinforce foundational arithmetic operations, while Tasks 3 and 4 require complex reasoning. For tasks 1 and 2, students should be encouraged to place lines between each number that represents a coded letter or underline each number that represents a letter. In addition, students should initially use a *symbol*, such as an *, &, ^, etc., as a *space* between words. You may want to provide the students with a template to use as a model.

Students who are ready for more advanced work can enrich Tasks 3 and 4 in several ways. First, they can use non-English languages to construct the messages to be sent. Second, they can use complex, multistep codes similar to those in Task 3. Third, they can use a computer spreadsheet to automatically encode and decode messages. Fourth, they can work with encoded messages of other students and attempt to decode them and determine the code rules that the other students are using. Although these tasks can be accomplished with groups, each student must provide individual work, to be evaluated.

If the students complete Tasks 1 through 4, enrichment tasks are provided at the end of the assessment. This adds an interesting angle to the assessment. An alphabet code sheet is provided at the end of the assessment for the students' use.

Required Materials
- Information on codes needed for enrichment tasks
- Code sheets
- Optional: templates for student's coded messages

Assessment Introduction: Here Is What You Will Do . . .

Secret agents have to communicate with each other using codes. Only people who know the code can understand what the messages mean. You will get to create your own messages, put them in a code, and decode the messages that your fellow secret agents send to you. If you do those jobs very well, your teacher may also ask you to create your own codes.

How do codes work? For this activity, a number represents each letter in the alphabet. For example, a simple code might look like this:

A = 1   B = 2   C = 3   D = 4

and so on.

But, if a code is too easy, then the other secret agents can find out what is in your secret messages. Your codes are going to be more difficult, so that only you and your teammates know how to decode your messages.

Prepare for tasks: Get into groups.

TASK 1: *Encode a Message*

Here are the steps you will follow:

- First, you will write your message. Make it at least two sentences long. You are going to give directions to the place where someone will meet you. For example, your message might say:
  "Meet me at my house at three o'clock on Saturday. It's next to the bakery on Main Street."

- Next, put your message away and fill out a code sheet, showing what numbers are equal to which letters of the alphabet. Have a number for all twenty-six letters. Use the following coding rules to write out this code on the Alphabet Code Sheet.

  A = 2
  B = the value you used for A, multiplied by 2
  C = the value you used for A, multiplied by 3
  D = the value you used for A, multiplied by 4

  and so on. You also need code numbers or symbols for spaces between words, and for numbers that you might use in addresses or phone numbers. Remember that you cannot use a number that has already been used for your letters. Write your code list on the Alphabet Code Sheet and label it "Task 1." Stop and have one of your partners check your work. Make sure that your code numbers are right!

- Now you have the message you wrote, and you have your code sheet. Change your message into numbers using this code. Write your coded message; use only numbers.

- Give JUST the coded message to one of your partners. Let him or her try to decode the message. Then see if he or she got it right.

- If your partner doesn't get the message decoded, see if you can figure out where the mistake is. DON'T do the decoding for your partner—just see if you can find the mistake. Write a note to your partner explaining why you think he or she got it wrong. If your partner figured out the code, write that down.

- Everyone in the group should have these five things to show the teacher:

  1. Your original message, written in words.
  2. Your Alphabet Code List that shows all of the letters and shows which code numbers go with each letter.
  3. Your encoded message, which looks like a number sentence.
  4. Your partner's effort to decode your message.
  5. Your note to your partner.

SCORING GUIDE—TASK 1

4   Exemplary

☐ Criteria for the Proficient category have been successfully completed.

☐ **More advanced work is completed. For example, the student recognizes the pattern in the code rule and explains it. The student explains how he or she decided on the numbers used for spaces and address numbers. Other examples of advanced work include:**

---

3   Proficient

☐ The message is at least two sentences long.

☐ The meaning of the message is clear and doesn't use any tricks.

☐ There are no spelling errors in the sentences.

☐ The numbers for each letter of the alphabet are calculated correctly.

☐ The partner's decoding is included.

☐ A note to the partner tells whether he or she figured out the code correctly, and tells what the error is, if any.

2   Progressing

☐ Four or five of the criteria in the Proficient category have been met.

☐ More work is needed.

1   Not meeting the standard(s)

☐ Less than four of the criteria in the Proficient category have been met.

☐ The task should be repeated.

TASK 2: *Make Up Your Own Code*

Now that you know how to use a secret agent code, it's time to write your own code.

Use these steps:

- First, write the math rule that you will use to create your code. For example,

$A = 2$	$D = C \times 3$	$G = F \times 2$
$B = A \times 3$	$E = D \times 2$	
$C = B \times 2$	$F = E \times 3$	

  and so on. Create any rule you want—and remember to keep it a secret from your fellow secret agents! Write the rule down on a piece of paper. Also, write the code list on the Alphabet Code Sheet and label this "Task 2."

- Using words, write a **message** with at least two sentences.

- Put the message in code. Write your message and your coded message on separate pieces on paper.

- Give JUST the coded message to one of your partners. Allow him or her to decode the message. Then see if he or she got it right.

- If your partner doesn't get the message decoded, see if you can figure out where the mistake is. DON'T do the decoding for your partner—just see if you can find the mistake. Write a note to your partner explaining why you think he or she got it wrong. If your partner figured out the code, write that down.

- Everyone in the group should have these five things to show the teacher:

  1. Your original message.

  2. Your coding rule and your alphabet code list showing all of the letters and numbers, and which code numbers go with each letter.

  3. Your encoded message.

  4. Your partner's effort to decode your message.

  5. Your note to your partner.

SCORING GUIDE—TASK 2

4   Exemplary

☐ Criteria for the Proficient category have been successfully completed.

☐ **Advanced work is completed. For example, the student uses at least two arithmetic operations to encode the message. The student identifies and explains the numerical pattern in his or her code. Other examples of advanced work include:**

_____

3   Proficient

☐ The coding rule uses one arithmetic operation.

☐ The message is at least two sentences long. The meaning of the message is clear and doesn't use any tricks. There are no spelling errors in the sentences.

☐ The numbers for each letter of the alphabet (code list) are calculated correctly. The partner's decoding is included.

☐ A note to the partner tells whether he or she figured out the code correctly, and tells what the error is, if any.

2   Progressing

☐ Three of the criteria in the Proficient category have been met.
☐ More work is needed.

1   Not meeting the standard(s)

☐ Less than three of the criteria in the Proficient category have been met.
☐ The task should be repeated.

If you need to do more work on the first two tasks, that's OK. It's important to understand how to use the math rule to get the codes and how to use them to make codes. Your teacher might ask you to do these tasks again. Only go on to the next task if your teacher says that it's OK.

TASK 3: *Make Another Code*

Here is what you will do: You are going to write codes again, but this time you have to give directions to another secret agent using a map. You can choose any map you want—city, state, national, or world map. In your message, describe where you want the secret agent to go. He or she is starting at your school. You have to tell him or her how many miles or kilometers to go and in what direction to travel. For example, your message might say, "Meet me in New York City. From our town, you have to travel 2,380 miles to the east." Decide on what measurement you will use. Use your map and the scale on the map to determine the direction and distance you will use in your message.

Here are the specific steps you need to follow:

- Create your own **code**, but use a different code than you did earlier in this activity. First, write the math rule that you will use to create your code. For example, A = 2, then B = A × 3, and so on. Create any rule you want—and remember to keep it a secret from your partners! Only you know the code.

- Write down the **rule** on a piece of paper. Now write the code list on an Alphabet Code Sheet and label it "Task 3."

- Using letters, write a **message** that has clear and accurate directions—remember to use both direction and distance in your message.

- Put this message into code. Write your message and your coded message on separate pieces of paper.

- Give your coded message to one of your partners. See if he or she can decode the message. If the message is not decoded, see if you can figure out where the mistake is. DON'T do the decoding for your partner—just see if you can find the mistake. Write a note to your partner explaining why you think he or she got it wrong. If your partner figured out the code, write that down.

- Everyone in the group should have these five things to show the teacher:
    1. Your original message, along with the map that you used for your directions.
    2. Your coding rule and your alphabet code list, showing all of the letters and numbers, and which code numbers go with each letter.
    3. Your encoded message.
    4. Your partner's effort to decode your message.
    5. The note to your partner.

SCORING GUIDE—TASK 3

4   Exemplary

☐ Criteria for the Proficient category have been successfully completed.

☐ **More advanced work is included. For example, the work clearly explains the relationship of the scale to the distance described in the message. The coding rule uses at least two arithmetic operations. Other examples of advanced work include:**

_____

3   Proficient

☐ The distance and directions are accurate.

☐ The coding rule uses at least one arithmetic operation.

☐ The message is at least two sentences long and has no errors.

☐ The code list is completely accurate.

☐ The partner's decoding is included, and the student accurately evaluates whether or not the decoding is correct.

2   Progressing

☐ Four of the criteria in the Proficient category have been met.

☐ More work is needed.

1   Not meeting the standard(s)

☐ Less than four of the criteria in the Proficient category have been met.

☐ The task should be repeated.

Only go on to the next task if your teacher says that it's OK.

TASK 4: *Harder Codes With Multisteps*

The problem with some secret agent codes is that the other secret agents are just as smart as you are! This means that the best secret agents always have to invent codes that are hard for other agents to decode.

You have already done "single-step" codes. In those codes, each letter was the same as one number. Now you are going to figure out a more complicated code system, where each code will require more steps. If you know about more advanced math operations, such as exponents, this is a good time to use them. Remember, the more complicated your message, the harder it will be for the other agents to figure it out!

How do you make a "multistep" code? The rule that you write has to have more than one step for each letter. In addition, the code might change from day to day. For example:

A = today's day of the month.
For example, if today were October 3, A would be equal to 3.

B = A^2 In this example, B would be equal to 3 $\times$ 3, or 9.

C = A^2 +1
D = A^2 + 2, and so on.

Remember that the value of these letters would change with every day. For example, on October 4, A would be equal to 4.

In this problem, you're going to give directions again. This time you don't know if the other secret agent knows about the metric system, so you're going to have give directions in both miles **and** kilometers.

Here are the steps you need to follow:

- Write down the **rule** on a piece of paper. Now write the code list on an Alphabet Code Sheet and label it "Task 4."

- Write a **message** that has clear and accurate directions. Remember to use both direction and distance in your message, then put the message in code. Write your message and your coded message on separate pieces of paper.

- Now give your coded message to one of your partners. See if he or she can decode the message. If the message isn't decoded, see if you can figure out where the mistake is. DON'T do the decoding for your partner—just see if you can find the mistake. Write a note to your partner explaining why you think he or she got it wrong. If your partner figured out the code, write that down.

- Everyone in the group should have these five things to show the teacher:

  1. Your original message, along with the map that you used for your directions (both miles and kilometers).

  2. Your coding rule and your alphabet code list, showing all of the letters and numbers, and which code numbers go with each letter.

  3. Your encoded message.

  4. Your partner's effort to decode your message.

  5. The note to your partner.

SCORING GUIDE—TASK 4

4 Exemplary

☐ Criteria for the Proficient category have been successfully completed.

☐ **More advanced work is included. For example, the work clearly shows the relationship of the scale to the distance described in the message. The coding rule uses at least two arithmetic operations. Other examples of advanced work include:**

---

3 Proficient

☐ The distance and directions are accurate.

☐ The coding rule uses at least one arithmetic operation that is different from the earlier tasks.

☐ The message is at least two sentences long.

☐ The meaning is understandable.

☐ The words are spelled correctly.

☐ The code list is completely accurate.

☐ The partner's decoding is included, and the student accurately evaluates whether or not the decoding is correct.

2 Progressing

☐ Five or six of the criteria in the Proficient category have been met.

☐ More work is needed.

1 Not meeting the standard(s)

☐ Less than five of the criteria in the Proficient category have been met.

☐ The task should be repeated.

ENRICHMENT TASKS

If you completed all four tasks and you would like additional interesting work about codes, talk with your teacher about the following ideas:

1. Use a computer spreadsheet to make your code list, and automatically encode and decode messages.

2. Read more about the use of codes by secret agents. Many important events in history, including the development of the atom bomb, the Civil War, and the German attacks on England, were all at the center of fascinating stories about the use of codes by secret agents.

3. Take some of the codes that your classmates have developed and look JUST at the coded numbers—NOT at the code list. Working JUST with the coded numbers, try to figure out what the message is and what the math rule is.

4. Write a story about the use of codes as a secret agent. Use some of your coded messages as part of the story.

5. What about real codes today? The CIA won't just tell you what they are! But real codes are sometimes also based on time. That is, at 10:02, A = 2, but at 10:03, A = 4. Both you and person receiving the code have to have very, very accurate clocks for this to work. Can you develop a code like this?

Alphabet Code Sheet

Your Name _____
(Sample)

Task Name or Number_____

Letter	Code No. 1		Code No. 2	
	Code Value	Rule	Code Value	Rule
A				
B				
C				
D				
E				
F				
G				
H				
I				
J				
K				
L				
M				
N				
O				
P				
Q				
R				
S				
T				
U				
V				
W				
X				
Y				
Z				

References

Ainsworth, L. 2003a. *Power standards: Identifying the standards that matter the most.* Englewood, Colo.: Advanced Learning Press.

Ainsworth, L. 2003b. *Unwrapping the standards: A simple process to make standards manageable.* Englewood, Colo.: Advanced Learning Press.

Bafile, C.L. January 13, 2003. "Making parents part of the 'in-volved' crowd." *Education World.* http://www.education-world.com/a_curr/profdev035.shtml.

Bafile, C.L. March 23, 2004. "Homework study hall: Mandatory 'make up' for missed work." *Education World.* http://www.education-world.com/a_admin/admin/admin347.shtml.

Bafile, C.L. August 9, 2004. "Teacher feature: Dotti Etzler." *Education World.* http://www.education-world.com/a_curr/teacher_feature/teacher_feature040.shtml.

Bafile, C.L. October 13, 2006. "Morning check-in paves the way for a great day." *Education World.* http://www.education-world.com/a_curr/teacher_feature/teacher_feature129.shtml.

Bafile, C.L. October 2007. "Ballentine Elementary goes to 'work' in many ways." *Education World.* http://www.educationworld.com/a_admin/partners/partners026.shtml.

Bafile, C.L. January 8, 2008. "Mystery readers keep kids in suspense." *Education World.* http://www.educationworld.com/a_curr/teacher_feature/teacher_feature169.shtml.

Barton, Paul E., and Richard J. Coley. 2007. *The family: America's smallest school.* Princeton, N.J.: Policy Information Center–Educational Testing Service.

Briggs, Tracey Wong. April 18, 2007. "Kindergartners enter a world of discovery." *USA Today.*

Candler, Laura. "How many ways are you smart?" (inventory). Teaching Resources: www.lauracandler.com.

Coleman, J. S., E.Q. Campbell, C.J. Hobson, J. McPartland, A.M. Mood, F.D. Weinfeld, and R.L. York. 1966. *Equality of educational opportunity.* Washington, D.C.: U.S. Government Printing Office.

Crouse, Amy, and Mike White. Spring/Summer 2008. "Teachers talk about teaching." *Ohio ASCD Journal* 11(2): 2, 30, 31.

Dufour, R., and R. Eaker. 1998. *Professional learning communities at work.* Bloomington, Ind.: National Education Service.

Educational Testing Service. 2007. "The family: America's smallest school report." Princeton, N.J.: Policy Information Center.

Education World. "Templates." http://www.education-world.com/tool_templates/index.shtml.

Gardner, Howard. 2006. Multiple intelligences: New horizons in theory and practice. New York: Basic Books.

Gitomor, Drew. 2007. "Teacher quality in a changing policy landscape: Improvements in the teacher pool." Princeton, N.J.: Policy Information Center–Educational Testing Service.

Goleman, D., R. Boyatzis, and A. McKee. 2002. *Primal leadership: Realizing the power of emotional intelligence.* Boston: Harvard Business School Press.

Haycock, K., Jackson, Mora, Ruiz, Robinson, and Wilkins. 1999. *Dispelling the myth*: High poverty schools exceeding expectation. Washington, D.C.: The Education Trust.

Intervention Central. "Charting Student Behavior." http://www.interventioncentral.com.

Jacobs, Heidi Hayes. 1997. *Mapping the big picture: Integrating curriculum and assessment K-12.* Alexandria, Virginia: Association for Supervision and Curriculum Development.

Kohn, Alfie. 1999. The schools our children deserve; Moving beyond traditional classroom and tougher standards. New York: Houghton Mifflin Company.

Kohn, Dwayne, "Mr. Kindergarten." http://www.misterkindergarten.com/.

Learning 24-7. April 7, 2005. "Classroom observation study." Las Vegas, Nevada: National Conference on Standards and Assessment.

Marzano, Robert. 2003. *What works in schools: Translating research into action.* Alexandria, Virginia: Association for Supervision and Curriculum Development.

Marzano, Robert J. 2007. *The art and science of teaching; A comprehensive framework for effective instruction.* Alexandria, Virginia: Association for Supervision and Curriculum Development.

Microsoft Office Online. "Templates." http://office.microsoft.com/en-us/templates/default.aspx.

Morse, G. June 2005. "Hidden harassment." *Harvard Business Review*: 28-30.

Reeves, Douglas B. 2004a. *Accountability in action: A blueprint for learning organizations*, 2nd Edition. Sample chapters are available for free at the Web site: www.MakingStandardsWork.com.

Reeves, Douglas B. 2004b. *Making standards work; How to implement standard-based assessments in the classroom, school, and district.* Englewood, Colo.: Advanced Learning Press.

Reeves, Douglas B. 2004c. "The case against the zero." *Phi Delta Kappan* 86(4): 324-325. Available as a free download at LeadandLearn.com.

Reeves, Douglas B. 2005. *101 questions and answers about standards assessment and accountability.* Englewood, Colo.: Advanced Learning Press.

Reeves, Douglas B. 2006. *The learning leader: How to focus school improvement for better results.* Alexandria, Virginia: Association for Supervision and Curriculum Development.

Reeves, Douglas B. 2008a. "Leading to change: Effective grading practices." *Educational Leadership* 65(5):85-87.

Renz, Heather. "Mastery Club." http://www2.redmond.k12.or.us/mccall/renz/masteryclub.htm.

Schmidt, W. H., C.C. McKnight, and S.A. Raizen. 1996. Splintered vision: An investigation of U.S. science and mathematics education: Executive summary. Lansing, Mich.: U.S. National Research Center for the Third International Mathematics and Science Study, Michigan State University.

Schmoker, Mike. 2006. *Results now: How we can achieve unprecedented improvements in teaching and learning.* Alexandria, Virginia: Association for Supervision and Curriculum Development.

Wiggins, G., and J. McTighe. 1998. *Understanding by design.* Alexandria, Virginia: Association for Supervision and Curriculum Development.

Wong, Harry K., and Rosemary Wong. 1991. The first days of school. Sunnyvale, Cal.: Harry T. Wong Publications.

Zattura Sims-El. September 23, 2006. "Closing Achievement Gaps Through Powerful Parenting." Diversity in Education Conference, Aiken Public School District, South Carolina.

Index